Control Modes on Mobile Software Platforms

Tobias Goldbach

Control Modes on Mobile Software Platforms

Empirical Studies on the
Importance of Informal Control

Tobias Goldbach
Darmstadt, Deutschland

Dissertation Technische Universität Darmstadt, 2016

D17

ISBN 978-3-658-14892-8   ISBN 978-3-658-14893-5 (eBook)
DOI 10.1007/978-3-658-14893-5

Library of Congress Control Number: 2016945150

Springer Vieweg

Printed on acid-free paper

This Springer Vieweg imprint is published by Springer Nature
The registered company is Springer Fachmedien Wiesbaden GmbH

Abstract

Over the past few years, software platforms and their corresponding ecosystems have gained a growing importance in the software industry. Especially mobile platforms such as Apple's App Store or Google's Android Market have offered novel ways to develop and distribute software. However, it is a challenge for platform providers to find the right balance between ensuring the platform's integrity while offering enough freedom to encourage third-party developers' motivation and innovation. Control theory, with its formal and informal control modes, is a suitable framework for describing and analyzing such coordination phenomena between two parties. Although there have been several Information Systems (IS) research calls regarding how and why control modes affect third-party developers' outcomes and behaviors on software platforms, limited research has been conducted in this context. Only little attention has been paid to informal control modes (self- and clan control), which have been previously found to be of particular importance in decentralized and complex multi-project settings such as software platforms.

Against this backdrop, this thesis presents three studies across four articles conducted to investigate how control modes affect third-party developers' crucial development outcomes and behaviors, how these effects may be explained and how promising control modes may be facilitated. The first two studies draw on control theory and self-determination literature. Within the first study, a laboratory experiment reveals how self-control compared to formal controls has consistently stronger effects on developers' app quality and intention to stay on a platform. Additionally, the study shows that these effects are explainable with developers' higher autonomy perception under self-control. In a field survey, the second study focuses on the role of third-party developers' intrinsic motivation, which mediates the positive effects of self-control and clan control on developers' work efforts and intention to stay on a platform. By combining control theory and social capital theory, the third study examines in another field survey how in particular clan control could be facilitated in order to enhance third-party developers' project performance and app success. The findings demonstrate that each social capital dimension (i.e., structural, cognitive and relational) positively affects the exercise of clan control, which in turn enhances developers' project performance and app success.

Overall, the thesis highlights the importance of informal control modes on software platforms regarding their positive effects on third-party developers' outcomes and behaviors. The conducted studies could demonstrate how self-control and clan control positively affect developers' outcome performance, app quality and intentions to stay on software platforms. Moreover, the findings shed light on the underlying explanatory mechanisms of why informal control modes can be exercised effectively on software platforms and how especially clan control may be facilitated with developers' social capital. By demonstrating how and why control modes operate on software platforms, this thesis answers to several calls for research in platform governance and IS control literature, and lays the foundation for further studies in this context. Platform providers may use the results to better understand how and why control modes affect third-party developers' outcomes and behaviors. They are advised to increasingly exercise informal control modes and find areas where such forms of control are applicable. Third-party developers may choose software platforms with more open, self-regulating and clan-based governance structures, in which they are able to benefit from their higher autonomy and freedom for intrinsic motivation.

Zusammenfassung

In den letzten Jahren haben Software-Plattformen und die dazugehörigen Ökosysteme an Bedeutung in der Software-Industrie gewonnen. Vor allem mobile Plattformen wie Apples App Store und Googles Android-Markt habe neue und gewinnbringende Wege für die Entwicklung und den Vertrieb von Software ermöglicht. Allerdings stehen Plattformanbieter vor der Herausforderung, die richtige Balance zu finden zwischen der Sicherstellung der Plattformintegrität und der Zulassung von Freiheiten für Dritt-Entwickler, um deren Motivation und Innovation zu fördern. Die Control-Theorie (oder auch Kontroll- und Steuerungstheorie) mit ihren formalen und informalen Control-Modi (englisch: formal and informal control modes) ist ein geeigneter Bezugsrahmen, um Dynamiken zwischen zwei Parteien zu beschreiben und zu analysieren. Trotz mehrerer Forschungsaufrufe zur Untersuchung von Control-Auswirkungen auf Ergebnisse und Verhaltensweisen von externen Entwicklern wurden bisher kaum Studien in diesem Kontext durchgeführt. Noch weniger Aufmerksamkeit wurden Informal Control Modes (unterteilt in Self-Control und Clan Control) gewidmet, denen in vorangegangen Studien besondere Bedeutung in Situationen mit dezentralisierten und komplexen Multi-Entwicklungsprojekten, wie auf Software-Plattformen vorzufinden, zugeschrieben wurde.

Vor diesem Hintergrund umfasst diese Dissertation drei Studien, die über vier Artikel veröffentlicht wurden. Die Studien wurden durchgeführt, um zu beantworten, wie sich Control-Mechanismen auf die Ergebnisse und das Verhalten von externen Entwicklern auswirken, wie diese Auswirkungen zu erklären sind und wie erfolgsversprechende Control Modes zusätzlich gefördert werden können. Die ersten beiden Studien greifen auf die Control-Theorie und die Selbstbestimmungstheorie zurück. Innerhalb der ersten Studie konnte mit einem Laborexperiment gezeigt werden, dass Self-Control stärkere positive Auswirkungen auf die App-Qualität der Entwickler sowie auf deren Absicht auf der Plattform zu bleiben hat, als im Vergleich zu Formal Control. Zusätzlich konnte die Studie darlegen, dass diese Auswirkungen durch eine höhere wahrgenommene Autonomie der Entwickler unter Self-Control erklärt werden kann. Die zweite Studie untersucht die Auswirkungen von Self-Control und Clan Control in einer Online-Umfrage mit App-Entwicklern und konnte positive Effekte auf die Anstrengungen der Entwickler und deren Absicht auf der Plattform zu bleiben aufzeigen. Dies konnte durch die intrinsische Motivation der Entwickler erklärt werden. Die dritte Studie kombiniert die Control-Theorie und die Sozialkapitaltheorie miteinander und untersucht in einer weiteren Feldstudie, wie insbesondere die Ausübung von Clan Control unterstütz werden kann, um die Projektperformance und den App-Erfolg der Entwickler zu steigern. Die Ergebnisse zeigen, dass alle drei Dimensionen von Sozialkapital (strukturelle, kognitive und relationale Dimension) eine positive Auswirkung auf Clan Control haben, was wiederum die Projektperformance und den App-Erfolg der Entwickler steigert.

Zusammengenommen offenbart die vorliegende Dissertation die Wichtigkeit von Informal Control Modes auf Software-Plattformen, insbesondere bezüglich deren positive Auswirkungen auf Ergebnisse und Verhaltensweisen der Entwickler. Die vorgestellten Studien konnten zeigen, wie Self-Control und Clan Control einen positiven Einfluss auf die Entwickler haben, u.a. auf deren Ergebnisperformance, App-Qualität und Absicht auf der Plattform zu bleiben. Zusätzlich legt die Dissertation dar, warum Informal Control Modes effektiv auf Software-Plattformen eingesetzt werden können und wie vor allem die Ausübung von Clan Control durch das Sozialkapital der Entwickler gestärkt werden kann. Damit antwortet die vorliegende Dissertation auf verschiedene Forschungsaufrufe bezüglich Plattform-Governance und der Control-Theorie und legt zudem ein Fundament für zukünftige Studien in diesem Kontext. Plattformanbieter können die Ergebnisse der Dissertation nutzen, um besser zu verstehen, wie und warum Control Modes auf Software-Plattformen die Ergebnisse und Verhaltensweisen von externen Entwicklern beeinflussen. Plattformanbietern wird empfohlen, vermehrt Informal Control Modes einzusetzen und entsprechend passende Bereiche für solche Control-Formen auf der Plattform zu finden. Externe Entwickler sollten für ihr Entwicklungsvorhaben Plattformen mit mehr Offenheit sowie selbstregulierende und Clan-basierte Governance-Strukturen wählen, um von ihrer gesteigerten Autonomie und Freiheit für intrinsische Motivation profitieren zu können.

Acknowledgments

This thesis was written during my time as a research assistant at the Chair of Information Systems & E-Services at the Technical University of Darmstadt. The completion of my dissertation was only possible with the support of many people, whom I sincerely want to thank.

Foremost, I especially would like to thank my supervisor Prof. Dr. Alexander Benlian for guiding me throughout my dissertation. His insights, advices and continuous support were greatly valuable in all the different phases and are very much appreciated. Additionally, I thank Prof. Dr. Peter Buxmann for co-supervising my dissertation.

I thank all of my colleagues, friends and students at the university with whom I had many fruitful discussions, who helped me with data collection and programming tasks and who provided me valuable feedback on ideas and articles. One study was conducted and published together with my colleague Viktoria Kemper, whom I want to thank in particular. I also gratefully acknowledge and thank the House of IT e.V. and the Software AG Darmstadt for supporting my work with a scholarship.

Finally, I want to thank my parents, family and friends for accompanying me on this journey. My deepest gratitude goes to my beloved partner. Her encouragement when times got rough and her unconditional support in many ways are much appreciated.

Darmstadt, 2016   Tobias Goldbach

Table of Contents

List of Tables

List of Figures

List of Abbreviations

AVE   Average Variance Extracted

CFI   Comparative Fit Index

CI   Confidence Interval

FC   Formal Control

IEEE   Institute of Electrical and Electronics Engineering

IS   Information System(s)

IT   Information Technology

LISREL   Linear Structural Relations

OS   Operating System

PLS   Partial Least Squares

SEM   Structural Equation Modeling

SD   Standard Deviation

SDK   Software Development Kit

RMSEA   Root Mean Square Error of Approximation

RQ   Research Question

SC   Self-Control

SRMR   Standardized Root Mean Square Residual

Chapter 1: Introduction

1.1 Motivation and Research Questions

More and more organizations in the software industry offer their products and services as systems consisting of complementary components created by independent external vendors, unlike traditional standalone systems formed by organizations itself (Burkhard et al. 2012; Tiwana et al. 2010). By opening organizational boundaries and by providing programming interfaces and developer tools, such organizations enable third-party developers to extent the core functionality of a software platform and to distribute applications via the platform marketplace to customers (Boudreau 2012). Such software platform ecosystems allow platform providers to build on external expertise and skills beyond the organizations' capabilities (Ceccagnoli et al. 2012), in order to respond to competitions and user needs in dynamic software ecosystem markets (Boudreau and Lakhani 2009; Katz and Shapiro 1994). Prominent examples of prospering and profitable platform ecosystems are Apple's App Store or Google's Android Market. By the end of 2014, Google's Play Store has offered over 1.43 million apps, published by nearly 400,000 developers (AppFigures 2015). Apple's iOS developers have earned a total of $25 billion from their app sales since the release of the platform in 2008 (Apple 2015) and shipments of smartphones worldwide have grown by 27.7% in 2014 to 1.3 billion (IDC 2015).

Compared to traditional software development contexts, software platforms are distinct in numerous ways and are therefore challenging platform owners and existing IS governance literature alike. First, third-party developers act merely autonomously and largely make their own decisions without being formally employed by the platform vendor resulting in a less hierarchical and less compulsory relationship (Gulati et al. 2012; Tiwana 2014). Second, the vast number of third-party applications and developers (e.g., 1.43 million apps in Google's Play Store from 400,000 active developers) makes it extremely cost and time consuming to observe and exercise tight control on each development project. Third, interests and goals of platform owners and third-party developers are not necessarily incongruent (Tiwana et al. 2010), given that both parties for example aim for increasing the platform's customer base to maximize app downloads and revenue (Boudreau 2012). Finally, according to platform governance literature, platform governance requires a balance of control for retaining the platform's integrity and objectives while simultaneously encouraging third-party developers' motivation and innovation (Tiwana et al. 2010). Platform Control is a central mechanism of platform governance (Tiwana et al. 2013) and control theory (Kirsch 1997; Ouchi 1980) has often been invoked in order to describe and analyze the alignment between two parties. Control Theory has a long tradition in IS research. However, due to its origination from early studies in organizational design and internal information technology (IT) projects (Kirsch 1997; Ouchi 1980), prior findings in IS control research may not be applicable in the context of software platform ecosystems. Nevertheless, various control mechanisms are currently exercised and observable on software platforms, which calls for profound investigations (Tiwana 2014).

Control is defined as a set of mechanisms a controller uses to influence controlees to act in accordance with the controller's objectives (Ouchi 1980) and can be categorized into formal and informal control modes (Kirsch 1997). Two research gaps are particularly noteworthy in IS control research. First, studies have largely focused on understanding the nature, antecedents and choice of formal and informal control modes (e.g., Choudhury and Sabherwal 2003; Chua et al. 2012; Henderson and Lee 1992; Kirsch 1996; Kirsch 1997; Kirsch et al. 2010; Kirsch et al. 2002) and only a few studies have analyzed the downstream effects of control modes. Studies that analyzed effects of control modes have focused almost exclusively on formal control modes and did not provide an explanatory argument why an effect occurs (Gopal and Gosain 2010; Keil et al. 2013; Tiwana 2010; Tiwana and Keil 2009). Studies investigating effects of informal control modes additionally resulted in mixed findings regarding the effects of clan control (Gopal and Gosain 2010; Tiwana 2010). Second, most IS control studies have either focused on internal projects (Cardinal 2001; Chua et al. 2012; Kirsch 1996; Kirsch 2004; Kirsch et al. 2010) or outsourcing projects (Gregory et al. 2013; Rustagi et al. 2008; Srivastava and Teo 2012; Tiwana and Keil 2009). Studies in more open settings have analyzed the relationship between general control and boundary resources on the Apple platform (Ghazawneh and Henfridsson 2013), or the relation between control and autonomy in a business technology ecosystem (Wareham et al. 2014). However, our knowledge regarding how control modes operate on software platforms, how they affect crucial outcomes and behavior of third-party developers and why such effects occur is still limited in IS research.

In order to contribute to the current research gaps regarding IS control on software platforms and platform governance literature, the primary goal of this thesis is to enhance our understanding regarding how different control modes operate in software platform ecosystem contexts. The thesis is guided by the three following overarching research questions:

RQ1: How do control modes on software platforms affect crucial third-party developers' outcomes and behaviors?

RQ2: Why do downstream effects of control modes on software platforms occur?

RQ3: How to facilitate critical control modes on software platforms?

In order to address these research questions, three empirical studies were conducted, published across four articles, analyzing how control modes operate on particularly mobile software platforms. The next section is devoted to the thesis research context and principal theories. It presents the fundamentals of software platform ecosystems and introduces the concepts of control theory. Following afterwards, the overall structure of the thesis is presented and summarized.

1.2 Theoretical Foundation

1.2.1 Software Platform Ecosystems

The overall thesis research contexts are software platform ecosystems with a particular focus on the mobile software industry. A platform in general refers to a collection of products and services that brings together groups of users in a two-sided market (Eisenmann et al. 2011). Software platforms in particular are defined as *"the extensible codebase of a software-based system that provides core functionality shared by the modules that interoperate with it, and the interfaces through which they interoperate"* (Tiwana et al. 2010, p. 675). In this regard, modules refer to add-on software which connects to the platform to add functionality, often called apps or extensions. A software platform is surrounded by its ecosystem which is defined as *"a set of actors functioning as a unit and interacting with a shared market for software and services, together with the relationship among them"* (Jansen et al. 2009, p. 35). Typical actors are often called hubs, niche players and customers (Iansiti and Levien 2004b), which in this thesis research context will be referred to as platform providers (or platform owners/vendors), third-party developers and platform users/customers (Tiwana et al. 2010). Platform owners deliberately open their organizations to enable third-party developers to develop and distribute apps for the platform and its customers (Boudreau 2012). Within such platform ecosystems, platform owners are able to utilize the expertise and skills of diverse third-party developers to create new capabilities and innovation (Ceccagnoli et al. 2012; Tiwana et al. 2010). Examples for software platform ecosystem in business-to-consumer settings are Apple's App Store, Google's Android Market or Microsoft's Windows Phone Store (Burkhard et al. 2012). Especially such mobile software platforms offer significant market opportunities due to continuous technology advances and vast market dynamics, which have led to numerous new actors as well as the re-positioning or disappearing of formally successful actors (Basole and Karla 2011).

Software platforms are typical two-sided markets in which two actors, i.e. third-party developers and platform users, represent one side of the market. Due to interactions between and within the two actors, typical network effects occur (Katz and Shapiro 1985; Rysman 2009). Therefore, more third-party developers on one side offering more apps will attract more platform users on the other side, while in turn more platform users will also attract more developers. Such network effects are inevitable for attaining a healthy and viable platform ecosystem, which means durability and growth for the platform (Hartigh et al. 2006). An ecosystem's health is constituted by a combination of productivity, robustness and niche creation, driven by the platform's output, variety, survival rate and persistent structure (Iansiti and Levien 2004b). Due to high market opportunities and dynamics, software platform are generally competing against each other over attracting and keeping customers and developers on board (Rochet and Tirole 2003). Platform owners attempt to integrate, keep and motivate third-party developers to produce high quality apps for the platform which contributes to positive network effects and therefore to a healthy and prospering software platform ecosystem (Hartigh et al. 2006; Rysman 2009). This thesis focuses on the side of third-party developers and the governance relation between platform owners and third-party developers.

Software platform ecosystem form a so-called meta-organization in which developers act merely in autonomous ways without being formal organizational employees (Gulati et al. 2012). A central governance challenge for platform owners is to relinquish enough control to encourage innovation by these mostly autonomous third-party developers while simultaneously retaining sufficient control to ensure the platform's integrity and objectives (Tiwana et al. 2010). In order to describe and study platform governance, Tiwana et al. (2010) suggest three perspectives, namely decision rights partitioning, sharing of ownership and platform control. Partitioning of decision right describes who (i.e., the platform owner or the third-party developers) has the authority and following responsibility to decide on specific aspects of the platform. These decisions could concern, for example, features and functionalities of the core platform and the modules, design concepts and user interfaces as well as the platform's interfaces. Ownership of a platform refers in a similar way to whether the platform is owned by a single firm or shared by all the ecosystems' actors. Finally, control is exercised by platform owners in order to achieve desirable outcomes and behaviors by third-party developers. Control theory as an essential part of platform governance provides the central theoretical lens for this thesis and is introduced in the next section.

1.2.2 Control Theory

Control theory has a long tradition in IS research, stemming from early studies in organizational design (Eisenhardt 1985; Ouchi 1979), marketing (Jaworski 1988) and information systems (Kirsch 1996; Kirsch 1997). Control theory is based on the assumption that goals of individuals are incongruent, which is why organizations attempt to find ways for controlling these individuals (Ouchi 1980). Broadly speaking, control is a managerial means to encourage individuals to behave in an aligned manner with the organizational purposes (Kirsch 2004; Ouchi 1979). Control is thus defined as attempts by one party (the controller) to influence and motivate an individual or a group of individuals (the controlee) to act in accordance with the controller's goals and objectives (Ouchi 1980). In the context of software platform ecosystems, the controller is the platform provider and the controlee is the collective of third-party developers who offer their apps on the platform.

Control is typically exercised via a variety of control mechanisms. The control framework by Ouchi (1979) and Kirsch (1997) is most prominently used in IS research for categorizing control mechanisms into formal and informal control modes (See Figure 1-1). Formal control modes rely largely on explicitly stated pre-specifications and contracts regarding performance targets and processes while informal control modes are a relational form of control, based on social skills and common norms and goals (Kirsch 1997; Ouchi 1980).

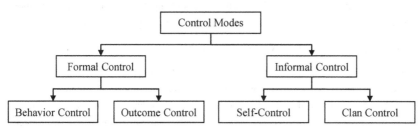

Figure 1-1: Types of Control Modes

On the one hand, formal control modes are divided into behavior control and outcome control. Outcome control refers to pre-determinations of desirable output requirements and performance targets of interim and final outputs as objectives without controlling the processes to achieve these outcomes. Pre-determined outcomes are then monitored, evaluated and accordingly rewarded. By contrast, behavior control refers to the pre-specification of procedures and methodologies while outcomes and their characteristics may be freely chosen by the controlee (Kirsch 1997; Ouchi 1980). Outcome control thus pre-specifies what should be accomplish and process control how outcomes should be achieved.

On the other hand, informal control modes are further divided into self-control and clan control. Self-control is predominantly exercised by controlees themselves, based on self-specification and self-monitoring, and by behaving in the best interest of the controller in a relational way (Kirsch 1997; Ouchi 1980). Controllers may provide an appropriate environment as well as tools and trainings for such self-regulation as well as being an example for desired behavior and outcome (Kirsch et al. 2002). Clan control refers to minimizing the differences between the two parties regarding their goals, strategies and visions. By promulgating shared values, beliefs and common goals, clan control leads to individuals who understand, share and commit themselves to such common norms and goals, which may ultimately result in enhanced processes and outcomes (Choudhury and Sabherwal

2003; Kirsch 1997; Ouchi 1980). Self- and clan control have been found to be particularly important when outcomes are unclear or difficult to measure and behavior is hard to specify or not observable (Kirsch 1996; Kirsch et al. 2002; Kohli and Kettinger 2004) such as in software platform contexts.

While this thesis' focus is on these broadly accepted and investigated control modes, other forms are worth mentioning. Cardinal (2001) introduced input control as another form of formal control, concerning the approval of financial and personal aspects for projects. Such input control in turn is also likely to influence activities and outcomes of a project. Studies in IS research, however, have largely neglected its investigation and measurements for input control are not yet developed. This thesis will incorporate input control into the identification of control modes on software platforms, while, however, omitting it for the empirical studies.

1.2.3 Thesis Positioning in IS Governance Research

Tiwana et al. (2013) proposed a framework for positioning and discussing governance studies in IS research, called the IT Governance Cube. The three cube dimensions represent who is governed, what is governed and how is it governed. According to Tiwana et al. (2013), previous research on who is governed have thoroughly focused on firm or interfirm levels while largely neglecting ecosystem arrangements. Further, the body of knowledge regarding what is governed is mainly concerning IT artifacts and stakeholders, with less focus on the governance of content. Finally, studies on how is governed have mainly analyzed with the lens of control theory and less via means of architecture or decisions rights. Moreover, the antecedents of government arrangements largely focused on the interaction of IT artifacts and firm levels and notably less at the governance of stakeholders in ecosystems. While the authors report a large body of knowledge on control theory in IS research, they also acknowledge that such research was almost exclusively conducted in combination with firm or interfirm contexts. They distinctly call for further research on control modes in massively distributed organizational contexts such as platform ecosystems, given the fundamental and challenging organizational shifts, which offer new and fertile research opportunities (Tiwana et al. 2013). In this respect, this thesis aims at contributing to the IS governance literature regarding stakeholder governance via control modes in platform ecosystems.

By doing so, this thesis also answers to other specific calls for research. Besides the aforementioned work of Tiwana et al. (2010, 2013), Wareham et al. (2014) highlights the lack of research on control mechanisms in technology ecosystems, in which purposefully designed governance mechanisms may promote the contributions of autonomous actors to create qualitative and profitable products and services. Further, Ghazawneh and Henfridsson (2013) investigates the balance between platform control and leveraging capabilities of third-party developers and discusses our limited understanding of control on such platforms. Lastly,

Tilson et al. (2012) reveal a paradox of control in digital infrastructure networks, which are similar to platform ecosystems, and call for further investigations on how control is exercised in such contexts.

1.3 Structure of the Thesis

In order to contribute to the principal research questions of the thesis, three studies were conducted, published across four scientific articles, which investigate control modes on software platforms with different foci and methodological approaches. The overall thesis is organized into six chapters. Following the introductory chapter, chapters 2 to 5 present the four published articles. These articles were slightly revised in order to achieve a consistent layout throughout the thesis. Figure 2 shows an overview of the chapters and articles.

The main focus of chapter 2 (article 1) is to describe, categorize and discuss occurring control mechanisms on actual mobile software platforms in order to gain a deeper understanding of control mechanisms and their application in such contexts. In addition to that, first results of a laboratory experiment are reported and described for a practitioner audience. The full article for the experimental study follows in chapter 3 (article 2) in which we analyzed the differential effects of formal and self-control on app developers' app quality, development effort and platform stickiness, and how these effects may be explained. Chapter 4 (article 3) investigates the effects of informal control modes on app developers' app quality, development effort and intention to stay in a real-life platform setting with a particular focus on the mediation role of third-party developers' intrinsic motivation. The study of chapter 5 (article 4) examines how third-party developers' social capital on software platforms may facilitate the exercise of clan control in order to enhance developers' project performance and app success. Finally, chapter 6 concludes the thesis with a summary of the key findings, contributions, limitations and opportunities for future research.

Following next, each chapter (i.e., article) is briefly summarized, including the main motivation and contributions to the research questions as well as the linkages between the articles. Given that the articles and corresponding studies were written and conducted with co-authors, first person plural (i.e., "we") is used throughout the thesis when applicable.

Chapter 2 (Article 1): The purpose of the first article is to lay out the basic understanding of which control mechanisms are actually exercised on software platforms. Therefore we investigated mobile software platforms from a third-party developer perspective, examining developer portals and communities in order to identify and categorize exercised platform control modes. We revealed that informal control modes (i.e., self- and control control) are predominantly exercised in Apples' App Store ecosystem as well as in Googles' Android Market. Additionally, we report first results of our experimental study, in which we compared differential effects of formal and self-control. This article therefore contributes to a basic understanding of control modes on software platforms as well as to research question *RQ1*.

Table 1-1: Thesis Structure and Overview of Articles

	Chapter 2	Control Modes on Software Platforms
Study 1	Article 1	Goldbach, T.; Benlian, A. (2015): Kontrollmechanismen auf Software-Plattformen. In: HMD - Praxis der Wirtschaftsinformatik, 52 (3), 347-357 (Goldbach and Benlian 2015c)
	Chapter 3	Formal vs. Self-Control on Software Platforms
	Article 2	Goldbach, T.; Kemper, V.; Benlian, A. (2014): Mobile Application Quality and Platform Stickiness under Formal vs. Self-Control — Evidence from an Experimental Study. In: International Conference on Information Systems (ICIS 2014), December 14-17, 2014, Auckland, New Zealand (Goldbach et al. 2014)
Study 2	Chapter 4	Informal Control and Intrinsic Motivation on Software Platforms
	Article 3	Goldbach, T.; Benlian, A. (2015): Understanding Informal Control Modes on Software Platforms – The Mediating Role of Third-Party Developers' Intrinsic Motivation. In: International Conference on Information Systems (ICIS 2015), December 13-16, 2015, Fort Worth, USA (Goldbach and Benlian 2015d)
Study 3	Chapter 5	Social Capital and Clan Control on Software Platforms
	Article 4	Goldbach, T.; Benlian, A. (2015): How Social Capital Facilitates Clan Control on Software Platforms to Enhance App-Developers' Performance and Success. In: International Conference on Information Systems (ICIS 2015), December 13-16, 2015, Fort Worth, USA (Goldbach and Benlian 2015b)
	Chapter 6	Conclusion

Chapter 3 (Article 2): Article 2 describes the experimental laboratory study in greater detail, which analyzes the differential effects of formal versus self-control mechanisms on crucial developer outcomes and behaviors. Traditional software development contexts are typically shaped by principal-agent relationships (Jensen and Meckling 1976) in which predominately formal control mechanisms are applied to make developers' activities and outcomes more transparent (Kirsch 1997; Ouchi 1979). Software-based platforms and their ecosystems are, however, distinct from traditional contexts (Tiwana et al. 2010) and research regarding the differential effects of control modes on third-party developers' outcomes and behaviors on software platforms and why such differences exist, is still scarce. We conducted a laboratory experiment in which we analyzed whether formal control by the platform provider or self-control by third-party developers leads to better outcomes and beneficial behaviors for a

software platform. During the experiment, participants were charged with the task to design an app for a simulated software platform while being exposed to different conditions (i.e., control modes). We used covariance-based structural equation modeling with Mplus for testing our theoretical model based on the collected data. First, the study results show that self-control is superior to formal control (i.e., outcome and behavior control) in ensuring higher app quality and in strengthening developers' intention to stay on the platform. Second, the study provides evidence that developers' perceived autonomy could serve as a mediator explaining why self-control leads to better developer outcomes and behaviors. Therefore, this study contributes largely to research question *RQ1* and *RQ2* by demonstrating which and why some control modes may be superior to other control modes in a software platform context.

The laboratory experiment provides strong internal validity by establishing a causal link in a controlled environment. However, the rather artificial characteristics of a laboratory experiment limit the external validity of the study. Therefore, the following studies were conducted as field surveys with app developers of real software platforms, for providing stronger external and ecological validity.

Chapter 4 (Article 3): The third article investigates the relationship between informal control modes and crucial third-party developer outcomes and behaviors with a focus on the mediation role of developers' intrinsic motivation to develop apps for a software platform. Previous studies have found that informal control mods (i.e., self-control and clan control) are particularly important in decentralized and complex multi-project settings (Goldbach et al. 2014; Kirsch 2004; Kohli and Kettinger 2004). Further, motivation is a well-studied and important factor influencing behaviors and outcomes (Locke and Latham 2004) and particularly intrinsic motivation has been found to be superior to other forms of motivation (Carton 1996; Deci and Ryan 2000), especially in more open environments (Ke and Zhang 2009). We therefore conducted an online survey with Android app developers to analyze how self-control and clan control affect third-party developers' intrinsic motivation and if developers' intrinsic motivation mediates the relationship between informal control modes and developers' effort, app quality and intention to stay on the platform. In order to analyze our hypothesis with the data, we used structural equation modeling with partial least squares in SmartPLS. The study results show that both self- and clan control positively influence third-party developers' intrinsic motivation. Further, the study indicates that developers' intrinsic motivation enhances developers' development effort, app quality and intention to stay on the platform. Finally, and more importantly, developers' intrinsic motivation serves as a mediator, carrying the positive effects of informal control modes over to developers' development effort and intention to stay on the platform. As such, the article contributes to research question *RQ1* and *RQ2*, showing how and why informal control affects third-party developers' behaviors and outcomes on actual software platforms with high external and ecological validity.

Given that we additionally found that clan control has stronger and more significantly effects on developers' intrinsic motivation and development effort compared to self-control, the following study investigates how exercising clan control on software platforms may be facilitated in order to further enhance developers' outcomes and behaviors.

Chapter 5 (Article 4): Article 4 analyzes how third-party developers' social capital facilitates the exercise of clan control on software platforms and how such clan control enhances developers' project performance and app success. Clan control has been previously found to be essential in complex it projects (Kirsch 2004; Kohli and Kettinger 2004) and especially important in more open and dynamic contexts (Kirsch et al. 2010). Exercising clan control relies heavily on social interactions and social relationships (Ouchi 1979), which could be analyzed with the theoretical framework of social capital (Nahapiet and Ghoshal 1998). We conducted a field survey with Android app developers in order to analyze how developers' social capital facilitates the exercise of clan control on software platforms and how clan control might enhance developers' performance and app success. For testing the theoretical model, we used partial least square structural equation modeling with SmartPLS. Our study demonstrates that each dimensions of social capital (i.e., structural, cognitive and relational social capital) positively affects the exercise of clan control and that successfully exercised clan control results in higher project performance and higher quality of the apps. Therefore, the study contributes to research question *RQ1* and *RQ3* by revealing how clan control could be facilitated in order to affect third-party developers' outcomes and behaviors.

In addition to the articles included in the thesis, the following articles were also published or submitted during my time as a PhD candidate within the thesis' project, which are, however, not part of the thesis:

- Goldbach, T.; Kemper, V. (2014): Should I Stay or Should I Go? The Effects of Control Mechanisms on App Developers' Intention to Stick with a Platform. In: Proceedings of the 22nd European Conference on Information Systems (ECIS 2014), June 9-11, Tel Aviv, Israel. (Goldbach and Kemper 2014)
- Goldbach, T.; Benlian, A. (2015): How Informal Control Modes affect Developers' Trust in a Platform Vendor and Platform Stickiness. In: Proceedings der 12. Internationalen Tagung Wirtschaftsinformatik 2015, 04-06 März, Osnabrück, Deutschland. (Goldbach and Benlian 2015a)
- Goldbach, T.; Benlian, A.: Relinquishing or retaining control? Understanding how control mechanisms affect application quality and developers' intention to stay on software platforms. (submitted journal article currently under review)

Chapter 2: Control Mechanisms on Software Platforms

Title: Kontrollmechanismen auf Softwareplattformen

Authors: Goldbach, Tobias, Technische Universität Darmstadt, Germany

Benlian, Alexander, Technische Universität Darmstadt, Germany

Published in: HMD - Praxis der Wirtschaftsinformatik, 52 (3), 347-357

Abstract

Software platforms, like the Apple App Store or Google Play, depend heavily on external app-developers who regularly develop and update apps for the platform. As part of platform governance, control theory can be invoked in order to describe and analyze the coordination between a platform vendor and app-developers. In this article we describe and categorize existing control mechanisms on software platforms and point out that Apple and Google largely exercise informal control (i.e., self- and clan control) and less formal control (i.e., input, process and output control). Additionally, in a lab experiment, we found evidence that self-control has more positive effects on the quality of developed apps and on developers' loyalty to the platform compared to formal control. The article demonstrates and suggests that platform vendors should increasingly focus on implementing informal control mechanisms.

Keywords Software Platforms, Platform Governance, Control Mechanisms, Formal and Informal Control

Zusammenfassung

Software-Plattformen, wie Apple App Store oder Google Play, sind stark von externen App-Entwicklern abhängig, die für Nutzer der Plattformen regelmäßig Apps erstellen und weiterentwickeln. Um die Koordination zwischen Plattformbetreiber und App-Entwickler zu beschreiben und zu analysieren, kann die Kontrolltheorie als Teil der Plattform-Governance herangezogen werden. In diesem Artikel werden eingesetzte Kontrollmechanismen auf Software-Plattformen zusammengetragen und klassifiziert. Wir legen dar, dass Apple und Google verstärkt auf informale Kontrollmechanismen (d. h. Selbst- und Klankontrolle) setzen und weniger auf formale Mechanismen (d. h. Zugangs-, Prozess- und Ergebniskontrolle). In einem Laborexperiment konnten wir außerdem aufzeigen, dass Selbstkontrolle im Vergleich zu formaler Kontrolle in Bezug auf die Qualität der entwickelten Apps und die Loyalität der Entwickler gegenüber der Plattform einen starken positiven Effekt ausüben kann. Der Artikel zeigt, dass Plattformbetreiber vermehrt informale Kontrollmechanismen einsetzen und einsetzen sollten.

Schlüsselwörter: Software-Plattformen,   Plattform-Governance,   Kontrollmechanismen, Formale und informale Kontrolle

2.1 Software-Plattform Ökosysteme

Software-Plattformen im Onlinekontext haben in den letzten Jahren die Software-Industrie bedeutend verändert. Unternehmen öffnen ihre Unternehmensgrenzen und ermöglichen externen Entwicklern den Software-Kern einer Unternehmensplattform um Funktionalitäten, Module oder Applikationen (Apps) zu erweitern (Tiwana et al. 2010). Die Unternehmen setzen dabei auf Wissen, Fähigkeiten und neue Ideen der externen Ressourcen, um schnellere Innovationszyklen zu generieren und um durch größeres Wachstum in den dynamischen Märkten konkurrenzfähig zu bleiben (Boudreau 2012). Apples App Store und Googles Android-Plattform werden durch externe Entwickler um Apps erweitert, Mozilla Firefox und Google Chrome um Browsermodule und auch kleinere Plattformen im TV-Sektor bieten externe Apps an. Um solche Plattformen herum entsteht ein eigenes Software-Ökosystem mit verschiedenen Akteuren, namentlich dem Plattformbetreiber, den externen Entwicklern und den Nutzern der Plattform (vgl. Figure 2-1) (Tiwana et al. 2010). Die verschiedenen Akteure interagieren miteinander und bringen eigene Vorstellungen und Ziele in das Ökosystem ein. Durch die offenen Strukturen entstehen neue Dynamiken und Chancen für Plattformbetreiber, aber auch neue Risiken und Herausforderungen.

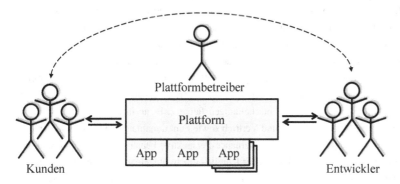

Figure 2-1: Akteure eines Software-Plattform Ökosystems

In der traditionellen Softwareentwicklung stellen Auftraggeber meist spezifische Vorgaben an Entwicklungsergebnisse und -prozesse, welche sie basierend auf Zwischenergebnissen und Protokollen überwachen und beeinflussen. Auf Software-Plattformen ist durch externe Entwickler und direkten Kundenkontakt die Softwareentwicklung allerdings anderen Dynamiken ausgesetzt (Tiwana 2014): Zunächst ist das Verhältnis zwischen Plattformbetreiber und Entwicklern weniger hierarchisch und weniger verbindlich. Entwickler sind nicht fest im Unternehmen des Plattformbetreibers eingebunden und können überwiegend eigene Entscheidungen treffen. Interessen und Ziele von Plattformbetreiber und externen Entwicklern sind nicht in allen Bereichen unterschiedlich. Meist zielen beide Akteure darauf ab, Kunden zufriedenzustellen und Umsätze zu erwirtschaften, z. B. durch innovative und hochwertige Apps. Letztlich ist es für Plattformbetreiber äußerst kosten- und zeitaufwendig jedes einzelne externe Projekt gewissenhaft zu überwachen und zu beeinflussen.

Für Plattformbetreiber ist es dennoch bedeutsam, die Dynamiken in Plattform-Ökosystemen zu steuern und zu kontrollieren sowie die unterschiedliche Zielsetzungen zu harmonisieren, um bestmögliche Ergebnisse aus Sicht des Betreibers und des Marktes zu erzielen. Für Unternehmen, die sich durch Öffnen ihrer Produkte für externe Entwickler zu einer Software-Plattform entwickeln möchten, stellt sich die Frage, welche Vorgaben spezifiziert werden sollten und welche Entscheidungen den externen Entwicklern überlassen werden können. Das Thema Plattform-Governance behandelt diese Fragestellung und wird im nächsten Kapiteln näher betrachtet.

2.2 Plattform-Governance und Kontrolltheorie

Aus Sicht der Plattform-Governance ist eine zentrale Herausforderung für Plattformbetreiber eine Balance zu finden zwischen genügend Freiheiten für externe Entwickler und ausreichend eigener Kontrolle und Steuerung über Aktivitäten auf der Plattform. Ersteres fördert Innovationen und Wachstum während letzteres die Integrität sowie Werte und Ziele der Plattform bewahrt. Plattform-Governance kann aus drei Perspektiven betrachtet werden (Tiwana et al. 2010): Die erste bezieht sich auf *Entscheidungsrechte* und wie diese unter den Akteuren der Plattform aufgeteilt werden. Wer ist autorisiert Entscheidungen zu treffen und übernimmt dafür Verantwortung? Entscheidungen fallen z. B. an in Bezug auf Design und Implementierung, Monetarisierung und Vertrieb sowie Funktionalitäten und Schnittstellen der Plattform und der Apps. Die zweite Governance-Perspektive behandelt das *Eigentumsrecht*. Gehört die Plattform allen Beteiligten oder lediglich einem einzelnen Unternehmen? Bleiben veröffentlichte Apps im Besitz der App-Entwickler oder geht das Eigentums- und Nutzungsrecht an den Plattformbetreiber über? Als dritte Perspektive nennen (Tiwana et al. 2010) die *Kontrolle auf Plattformen*. Kontrolle (Control) wird definiert als das Bestreben, Individuen zu motivieren, um gewünschte Ergebnisse zu erzielen (Ouchi 1979). Hierbei wird unterschieden zwischen einer Person bzw. einem Unternehmen, das Kontrolle ausübt (dem Controller) und einer Person bzw. Personengruppe, die der Kontrolle ausgesetzt ist (dem Controllee). In der Kontrolltheorie haben sich zwei Kategorien von Kontrollformen herauskristallisiert, namentlich formale Kontrolle und informale Kontrolle (z.B., Kirsch et al. 2002):

Formale Kontrolle basiert auf vertraglich festgehaltenen Regeln, einer regelmäßigen Überwachung der Einhaltung dieser Regeln und einer entsprechenden Belohnung bzw. Sanktionierung. Formale Kontrolle wird weiter unterteilt in Zugangskontrolle, Prozesskontrolle und Ergebniskontrolle. *Zugangskontrolle* (Input Control) regelt, wer oder was Zugang zu einem Unternehmen oder einem Projekt erhält. Eingesetzt wird Zugangskontrolle häufig in der Personalverwaltung, in der Kriterien zur Auswahl von Mitarbeitern festgelegt werden. Zur Zugangskontrolle gehört auch die Verteilung von finanziellen Mitteln oder sonstigen Ressourcen, die einem Projekt zur Verfügung gestellt werden und dadurch den weiteren Verlauf des Projektes beeinflussen. *Prozesskontrolle* (Process oder Behavior Control) dient der Steuerung von Aktivitäten und Handlungen der Kontrollierten. Hierzu gehören neben Verhaltensregeln oder Prozessstandards auch vorgeschriebene Entwicklungsmethoden. Nach der Spezifikation von Prozessvorgaben werden die Prozesse in der Regel auf Basis von Berichten und Protokollen überwacht und Mitarbeiter bezogen auf die Einhaltung dieser Vorgaben belohnt bzw. sanktioniert. *Ergebniskontrolle* (Output Control) kontrolliert die Zielerreichung eines Projektes. Dies umfasst z. B. technische, funktionale und visuelle Spezifikationen des Endproduktes sowie Kosten- und Zeitvorgaben. Ergebnisse werden anhand vordefinierter Metriken analysiert und ebenfalls entsprechend belohnt bzw. sanktioniert. Ergebniskontrolle spezifiziert nicht, mit welchen Methoden ein Ergebnis erreicht werden soll und umgekehrt werden unter Prozesskontrolle keine Anforderungen zur Erreichung der Endziele gestellt (Cardinal 2001; Kirsch et al. 2002).

Informale Kontrolle basiert auf sozialen und (zwischen-) menschlichen Strategien und ist unterteilt in Selbst- und Klankontrolle. Informale Kontrollmechanismen werden vor allem eingesetzt, wenn Prozesse und Ergebnisse nur schwierig oder sehr kostspielig überprüft und überwacht werden können sowie wenn gewünschte Prozesse und Ergebnisse nicht oder nur ungenügend bekannt sind. Mit *Selbstkontrolle* (Self-Control) ermöglicht ein Kontrolleur den Kontrollierten sich selbst zu organisieren, indem er z. B. das dafür notwendige Wissen und Methoden schult und entsprechende Hilfsmittel zur Verfügung stellt. Individuen werden dazu ermutigt, sich eigene Ziele zu setzten und eigene Methoden und Prozesse zu etablieren. Eine Belohnung bzw. Sanktionierung findet nach eigenem Ermessen statt. Hierdurch können vor allem neue Prozesse und Ergebnisse entstehen, die später als Standards übernommen werden. Mit *Klankontrolle* (Clan Control) schaffen Kontrolleure gemeinsame Werte und Normen sowie gemeinsame Ziele und Visionen. Hieraus entstehen Gruppen von Individuen, die gemeinsame Werte und Normen teilen und sich für gemeinsame Ziele einsetzen. Solch eine Gruppe tendiert zur Umsetzung ähnlicher Prozesse und Ergebnisse. Belohnungen und Sanktionen finden direkt oder indirekt durch die Gruppe und durch Gruppendynamiken statt. Eine direkte Überwachung ist durch den Kontrolleur nicht notwendig (Kirsch et al. 2002).

2.3 Kontrollmechanismen auf Apples App Store Plattform

Die Kontrolltheorie ist bereits weit in der Wirtschaftsinformatik-Literatur verbreitet, allerdings existieren bisher nur wenige Studien zu Kontrollformen auf Software-Plattformen (Tiwana 2014). Um ein Verständnis dafür zu bekommen, welche Kontrollmechanismen auf Software-Plattformen derzeit verwendet werden, betrachten wir im Folgenden den Apple App Store als Fallbeispiel. Die Firma Apple Inc. ist in den letzten Jahren insbesondere durch das iPhone und das iPad international bekannt und erfolgreich geworden. Nachdem 2007 das iPhone vorgestellt wurde, folgte 2008 der Apple App Store, welcher nur wenige Monate später für externe Entwickler geöffnet wurde. Über ein Software Development Kit (SDK) können Drittanbieter eigene Apps für das iPhone und iPad entwickeln und vertreiben. Apple berichtete Anfang dieses Jahres über 6 Mio. registrierte App-Entwickler und über 1,4 Mio. angebotene Apps (Apple 2015). Apple setzt an verschiedenen Stellen unterschiedliche Kontrollmechanismen ein, um die Prozesse und Ergebnisse der App-Entwickler zu beeinflussen. Nachfolgend werden Kontrollmechanismen beispielhaft aufgeführt (vgl. Table 2-1). Als Quellen dienten Analysen des Apple App Stores und des Apple Developer Portals (https://developer.apple.com/) sowie (Bergvall-Kåreborn and Howcroft 2011).

Table 2-1: Kontrollmechanismen auf Software-Plattformen

<table>
<tr><th></th><th>Kontroll-
form</th><th>Kurzbeschreibung</th><th>Beispiel Kontrollmechanismen:
Apple App Store</th></tr>
<tr><td rowspan="3">Formale</td><td>Zugangs-
kontrolle</td><td>Auswahl und Zulassung von (Personal-) Ressourcen</td><td>Eintrittsbarrieren für Entwickler: kostenpflichtige Registrierung und Bindung an Apple Hard- und Software</td></tr>
<tr><td>Prozess-
kontrolle</td><td>Steuerung und Überwachung von Verhalten und Aktivitäten</td><td>Bereitstellung von SDKs und Frameworks zur Programmierung und Veröffentlichung von Apps, Empfehlungen für Best-Practice Vorgehensweisen</td></tr>
<tr><td>Ergebnis-
kontrolle</td><td>Spezifikation und Über-prüfung von (End-) Ergebnissen</td><td>Veröffentlichung von Review und Interface Guidlines. Überprüfung und ggf. Ablehnung von eingereichten Apps. Nutzerbasierte Bewertungen und Bestenlisten von Apps</td></tr>
<tr><td rowspan="2">Informale</td><td>Selbst-
kontrolle</td><td>Ermöglichung und Förderung von Selbst-organisation</td><td>Freie Budget-, Zeit- und Personalplanung der Entwickler. Freie Auswahl und Umsetzung von App-Funktionalitäten</td></tr>
<tr><td>Klan-
kontrolle</td><td>Schaffung und Förderung gemeinsamer Werte, Normen und Ziele</td><td>Kommunikation von Werten, Normen und Zielen durch Produkte, Marketingkampagnen, Corporate Identity und die allgemeine Firmenpolitik</td></tr>
</table>

Zugangskontrolle Apple rekrutiert neue Entwickler nicht selbst, sondern hält seine Plattform für alle Entwickler offen, stellt hierbei allerdings einige Eintrittsbarrieren auf. Das Apple-Developer-Programm berechtigt zum Zugang zu bereitgestellten Entwicklungsressourcen und ermöglicht die Veröffentlichung von Apps im App Store. Eine Registrierung kostet $ 99 US-

Dollar und muss jährlich erneuert werden, veröffentlichte Apps werden sonst wieder aus dem App Store entfernt. Weiter stellt Apple für die Entwicklung von Apps Entwicklungswerkzeuge bereit. Diese können allerdings nur mit Mac OS X Geräten von Apple betrieben werden. Der Einstieg in die Apple App-Entwicklung setzt somit eine kostenpflichtige Registrierung und den Besitz von Apple Geräten voraus. Mit diesen Barrieren, bzw. beschränkter Plattformoffenheit (Benlian et al. 2015), stellt Apple u. a. sicher, dass Entwickler ernsthaft an der Entwicklung und Veröffentlichung von gewinnbringenden Apps interessiert sind.

Prozesskontrolle Die von Apple bereitgestellten Entwicklungswerkzeuge haben einen direkten und indirekten Einfluss auf die Entwicklungsprozesse der App-Entwickler. Mit der integrierten Entwicklungsumgebung XCode stellt Apple ein zentrales Werkzeug zur Verfügung, mit dem die Programmierung, das Testen und die Veröffentlichung von Apps durchgeführt werden kann. Daneben unterstützen das veröffentlichte SDK und weitere Frameworks sowohl bei der technischen als auch bei der visuellen Integration der Apps in die Plattform. Über das Developer Portal informiert Apple zusätzlich über Best-Practice-Vorgehensweisen im Implementierungsprozess und Lösungen zu typischen Problemen bei der App-Entwicklung. Die Verwendung dieser Entwicklerwerkzeuge und Frameworks ist zwar größtenteils freiwillig, dennoch mangelt es derzeit an gleichwertigen Alternativen. Durch die bereitgestellten Ressourcen beeinflusst Apple maßgeblich, auf welche Weise Apps entwickelt, getestet und veröffentlicht werden.

Ergebniskontrolle Apple setzt sowohl eine direkt als auch indirekte Ergebniskontrolle um. Über Allgemeine Geschäftsbedingungen behält sich Apple das Recht vor, unangebrachten und ungeeigneten Apps den Zugang zum App Store zu verweigern. Regelungen für den Zugang zum App Store sind in den Review Guidelines und den iOS Human Interface Guidelines hinterlegt. Dort befinden sich Hinweise zur technischen Umsetzung, zu Sicherheits- und Privatsphäre-Konfigurationen sowie zu Design und Interfaces der Apps. Im Falle einer Ablehnung nennt Apple allerdings keine Gründe und der Ablehnungsprozess bleibt folglich intransparent. Ebenfalls ist nicht bekannt, ob diese Kontrolle stichpunktartig oder für alle eingereichten Apps stattfindet. Neben der direkten Ergebniskontrolle etabliert Apple einige indirekte Mechanismen, um hochwertige und möglichst fehlerfreie Apps zu fördern. Hierzu gehören das nutzerbasierte Bewertungssystem und die Platzierung von beliebten Apps in Bestenlisten. App Bewertungen und Kommentare durch Benutzer beeinflussen die Qualitätssignale einer App sowie die Sichtbarkeit im App Store. Beliebte und erfolgreiche Apps können zudem von Apple für die Startseite ausgewählt und beworben werden. Durch diese Mechanismen entstehen für Entwickler zusätzliche Anreize, hochwertige und für die Benutzer zufriedenstellende Apps zu entwickeln. Eine Belohnung bzw. Sanktionierung findet in diesem Falle indirekt über den Markt statt.

Selbstkontrolle Trotz der zahlreichen Vorgaben, Richtlinien und Restriktionen sind externe Entwickler der Apple Plattform in vielen Punkten sich selbst überlassen. Im Vergleich zu Kontrollmechanismen in traditioneller Softwareentwicklung wird z. B. Budget-, Zeit- und Personalplanung durch die App-Entwickler selbstständig vorgenommen. Die Einhaltung von Veröffentlichungsterminen und Kostenstrukturen wird nicht von Apple überwacht und liegt in der Verantwortung der Entwickler. Ebenso haben Entwickler freie Hand bei der Auswahl und Umsetzung der funktionalen Implementierung ihrer Apps. Apple setzt hier bewusst auf die Ideen und Innovationen der externen Entwickler und fördert somit neue Projekte und das Wachstum der Plattform.

Klankontrolle Apples Werte und Normen werden vor allem in der allgemeinen Firmenpolitik und in den Produkten des Unternehmens deutlich. Apple Produkte wie iPhone und iPad haben gewisse Eigenschaft gemeinsam, welche die Werte des Unternehmens wiederspiegeln: Hohe Innovation, ein modernes Design, eingängige Nutzbarkeit, für manche Nutzer ein Statussymbol sowie eine einfache Integration der Produkte in das Apple-Ökosystem. Viele dieser Werte, Normen und Ziele von Apple werden durch Marketingkampagnen, die Corporate Identity und die Produkte nach außen getragen und von den Apple Kunden und App-Entwicklern verstanden, anerkannt und übernommen. Entwickler reproduzieren diese Eigenschaften in den Funktionalitäten und Designs ihrer Apps und schaffen einen Wiedererkennungswert des Apple-Ökosystems. Apple beeinflusst somit durch die Kommunikation der Unternehmenswerte die Prozesse und Ergebnisse der externen App-Entwickler.

Vergleich zur Android App-Entwicklung An dieser Stelle findet ergänzend ein Vergleich zu Kontrollmechanismen auf Googles Android Plattform statt. Die Android App-Entwicklung ist weniger restriktiv und setzt an vielen Punkten verstärkt auf Selbstkontrolle der Entwickler. Für Android-Entwickler fällt lediglich eine einmalige Registrierungsgebühr von $ 25 US-Dollar an. Dies stellt eine niedrigere Eintrittsbarriere im Vergleich zum Apple-Developer-Programm dar und erklärt möglicherweise die höhere Anzahl an Entwicklern und angebotenen Apps im Google Playstore. Durch das offenere und freiere System sind eine Vielzahl von Entwicklungs-, Design und Testumgebungen in der Android Community verfügbar und somit werden auch eine Vielzahl verschiedener Entwicklungsprozesse umgesetzt. Eine direkte Ergebniskontrolle findet nicht statt, da alle Apps im Google Playstore zugelassen werden. Lediglich nach Beschwerden von Kunden werden nachträglich unangemessene Apps entfernt, die etwa wichtigen Sicherheits- und Privatsphäre-Aspekten nicht gerecht werden. Bewertungssysteme sind ebenso vorhanden wie Best-Practice-

Implementierungen und Lösungen für gängige Probleme. Die Werte, Normen und Ziele der offenen Android-Plattformen spiegeln sich folglich in den eingesetzten Kontrollmechanismen wieder.

2.4 Laborexperiment zur Bedeutung von Selbstkontrolle

Um Auswirkungen verschiedener Kontrollmechanismen auf Software-Plattformen zu untersuchen, haben wir ein Laborexperiment in diesem Kontext vorbereitet und durchgeführt (Goldbach et al. 2014). Ziel war es zu untersuchen, ob gerade die auf Software-Plattformen weit verbreiteten Selbstkontrollmechanismen im Vergleich zu formaler Kontrolle zu hochwertigeren Apps führt und ob selbstorganisierte Entwickler eine Plattform dadurch eher weiterverwenden würden. Die Teilnehmer des Experiments nahmen die Rolle von App-Entwicklern einer fiktiven Software-Plattform ein. Der fiktive Plattformbetreiber gab vor, einen Mockup-Designer und neue Plattform-Vorgaben analysieren zu wollen. Die Teilnehmer hatten die Aufgabe eine App für eine ebenfalls fiktive deutsche Hotelkette mit Hilfe des Mockup-Designers (vgl. Figure 2-2) zu entwerfen.

Figure 2-2: Screenshot des Mockup-Designers

Die genaue Funktionalität und das Design der App waren hierbei frei bestimmbar. Die Teilnehmer wurden in drei Gruppen eingeteilt, die jeweils unterschiedlichen Kontrollformen ausgesetzt waren. Diese waren für formale Kontrolle die Gruppen Prozesskontrolle und Ergebniskontrolle und für informale Kontrolle die dritte Gruppe Selbstkontrolle. Die Kontrollmechanismen wurden in Form von Vorgaben des Plattformbetreibers umgesetzt. Die Teilnehmer wurden aufgefordert, diese Vorgaben einzuhalten und umzusetzen, da ihre entworfene App sonst nicht für den App Store zugelassen werden würde. Als zusätzliche

Motivation konnten die Teilnehmer ein Tablet gewinnen, sofern ihre App den Vorgaben entsprach. Die Gruppe Prozesskontrolle bekam Vorgaben zum Vorgehen bei der App-Entwicklung. Die Teilnehmer sollten beispielsweise zuerst einen Hintergrund auswählen, dann den Titel der App hinzufügen sowie anschließend ein Icon zur bildlichen Beschreibung auswählen. Zum genauen Design der App wurden allerdings keine Vorgaben angegeben. Die Gruppe Ergebniskontrolle bekam Vorgaben zum Erscheinungsbild der App. Beispielsweise sollte die App ein Icon in einer bestimmten Größe an einem bestimmten Platz, einen bläulichen Hintergrund sowie eine Navigationsleiste im unteren Bereich der App aufzeigen. In welcher Reihenfolge die Teilnehmer vorgehen, wurde dieser Gruppe freigestellt. Die dritte Gruppe Selbstkontrolle wurde aufgefordert, sich selbstständig zu organisieren, sich eigene Ziele zu setzen und nach eigenen Vorstellungen vorzugehen.

Die 138 Teilnehmer des Experiments waren Studierende einer großen deutschen Universität, überwiegend aus technischen Studiengängen mit Erfahrung in der Software- und App-Entwicklung und wurden mit 5 € pro Teilnehmer vergütet. An einem Rechner im PC-Labor wurden die Teilnehmer zunächst in den vorliegenden Plattformkontext eingewiesen und zufallsbasiert einer der drei Gruppen zugewiesen. Dann wurde den Teilnehmern der Mockup-Designer mit einem Video erklärt, mit dem verschiedene Design-Elemente per Drag & Drop auf die App-Bildschirme hinzugefügt, ausgerichtet und formatiert werden konnten. Zu den Elementen zählten z. B. Hintergrundfarben, Texte und Eingabefelder sowie eine Reihe von Icons und Bildern, außerdem App-spezifische Elemente wie Kalender, Chat und Videoplayer. Nach Ablauf der Entwurfszeit folgte ein Fragebogen bezogen auf die Absicht der Teilnehmer, die Software-Plattform auch in Zukunft weiter für App-Entwicklung zu verwenden und bezogen auf ihre wahrgenommene Autonomie während der Entwurfszeit. Beide Variablen wurden jeweils mit drei Fragen auf einer 5-Punkt-Likertskala erhoben. Im Anschluss an das Experiment wurden die entworfenen Apps in einer Expertenrunde bezüglich Ihrer Qualität, basierend auf den Merkmalen Funktionalität, Nützlichkeit, Bedienkomfort und Design, auf einer 6-Punkt-Likertskala bewertet.

Die Studie kam zu folgenden Ergebnissen (vgl. Figure 2-3): In der Gruppe Selbstkontrolle war die Absicht der App-Entwickler, die Software-Plattform auch in Zukunft für ihre App-Entwicklung zu nutzen, und damit die Loyalität der Entwickler, signifikant höher (d. h. um 15,7%) als in den Gruppen Prozesskontrolle und Ergebniskontrolle (zusammengefasst in der Kategorie „Formale Kontrolle"). Ähnlich war die Qualität der entworfenen Apps in der Gruppe Selbstkontrolle signifikant höher (d. h. um 16,4 %) als in den beiden anderen Gruppen. Aus theoretischer Sicht erklären wir diese Ergebnisse anhand der Theorie für Selbstbestimmung nach Deci and Ryan (2002).

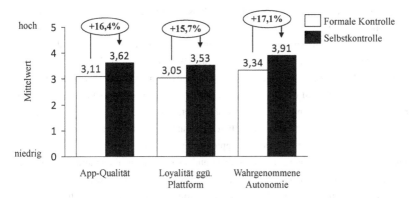

Figure 2-3: Ergebnisse des Experiments

Teilnehmer unter formalen Kontrollmechanismen sind Restriktionen ausgesetzt und müssen ihre Ideen und Ziele sowie ihr Vorgehen anpassen. Sie sind dadurch höherem Druck ausgesetzt, können weniger frei arbeiten und sind insgesamt weniger zufrieden mit ihrer Tätigkeit. Dies verringert auch die Absicht, weiterhin unter solchen Bedingungen zu arbeiten. Dies spiegelte sich in unserem Experiment darin wieder, dass Teilnehmer der Gruppe Selbstkontrolle ein signifikant höheres (d. h. um 17,1 %) Autonomiegefühl wahrgenommen haben. Die daraus folgende höhere intrinsische Motivation und höhere Identifikation mit der Tätigkeit und der App haben schließlich zu einem besseren Ergebnis geführt. Dies zeigte sich in unserer Studie in der signifikant höheren Qualität der entworfenen Apps. Zusammengefasst kann festgehalten werden, dass Selbstkontrolle nicht nur zu Entwicklern führt, die sich auf der Plattform wohler fühlen und die Plattform weiter nutzen möchten, sondern ebenfalls zu hochwertigeren besseren Ergebnissen dieser Entwickler. Der verstärkte Einsatz von Selbstkontrolle auf Software-Plattformen kann also einen wichtigen Beitrag leisten, Innovation und Wachstum zu fördern. Als Limitation der Studie ist die eher künstliche Umgebung des Experiments zu nennen, dessen Ergebnisse in zukünftigen Feldstudien weiter zu untersuchen sind. Erste Umfragen mit App-Entwicklern verifizieren jedoch die Experimentergebnisse bereits.

2.5 Erkenntnisse und Empfehlungen

Obwohl Software-Plattform Ökosysteme im Onlinekontext schon seit einigen Jahren erfolgreich im Markt etabliert sind und der Software-Industrie neue erfolgsversprechende Wege für die Entwicklung und Distribution von Software ermöglichen, ist die Literatur im Bereich der Kontrolle und Steuerung auf Software-Plattformen noch in den Anfängen. Wir konnten in diesem Artikel aufzeigen, dass auf Apples App Store Plattform und auch auf

Googles Android Plattform weniger strikte formale Kontrollmechanismen eingesetzt werden als in traditioneller Softwareentwicklung, dafür vermehrt informale Kontrollmechanismen. Bei den eingesetzten formalen Kontrollmechanismen wurde zudem deutlich, dass diese nicht in ihrer Reinform umgesetzt werden. Für die Prozesskontrolle bei Apple sind zwar einige Werkzeuge und Spezifikationen vorhanden, die den Entwicklungsprozess beeinflussen, diese müssen aber nicht zwingend eingesetzt werden. Ebenfalls ist bei der Ergebniskontrolle nicht ersichtlich, wie detailliert Apps vor der Freigabe untersucht werden. Weniger hierarchische Beziehungen und eine große Masse an Entwicklern und Projekten erschweren zudem eine strikte Ausführung formaler Kontrolle. Apple hat vor allem eine starke und präsente Klankontrolle, die sich in den eigenen Produkten und auch den Apps der externen Entwickler wiederspiegelt. Zudem konnten wir in unserem Laborexperiment zeigen, dass Selbstkontrolle im Vergleich zu formaler Kontrolle zu loyaleren Entwicklern und hochwertigeren Apps führen kann.

Plattformbetreiber und Unternehmen, die sich hin zu einem Plattform-Ökosystem entwickeln wollen, sollten sich explizit darüber Gedanken machen, in welchen Kontexten sie Vorgaben und Richtlinien spezifizieren möchten. Während einige kritische Themen wie Sicherheit und Privatsphäre-Einstellungen von Apps gewiss einer formalen Kontrolle bedürfen, um Nutzer zu schützen, zeigt unser Artikel, dass verstärkt informale Kontrollmechanismen eingesetzt werden können und sollten. Vor allem die selbstständige Organisation durch Selbstkontrolle kann Verhalten und Ergebnisse der Entwickler auf Software-Plattformen positiv beeinflussen. Ziel ist die Schaffung von Werten und Zielen, die gemeinsam verfolgt werden und weniger starker Kontrolle und Überwachung unterliegen. Möglich ist dies beispielsweise durch Trainings, Konferenzen und Zertifizierungen für Entwickler sowie Schulungen zur selbständigen Organisation. Es bleibt zu beobachten, wie sich die Entwicklung und der Vertrieb von Software weiter durch das Internet verändern werden. Wir glauben, dass durch die Öffnung der Unternehmensgrenzen und den Einsatz von nur wenigen formalen Kontrollmechanismen externe Potentiale und Innovationen bestmöglich genutzt werden können, um in den dynamischen Märkten konkurrenzfähig zu bleiben.

Chapter 3: Formal vs. Self-Control on Software Platforms

Title:　Mobile Application Quality and Platform Stickiness under Formal vs. Self-Control – Evidence from an Experimental Study[1]

Authors:　Goldbach, Tobias, Technische Universität Darmstadt, Germany

Kemper, Viktoria, Technische Universität Darmstadt, Germany

Benlian, Alexander, Technische Universität Darmstadt, Germany

Published in: International Conference on Information Systems (ICIS 2014), December 14-17, 2014, Auckland, New Zealand.

Abstract

Although control modes have been extensively studied in IS research, minimal research attention has been directed towards understanding how different control mechanisms operate in software-based platforms. Drawing on self-determination theory and IS control literature, we conducted a laboratory experiment with 138 participants in which we examined how well third-party developers contribute to a mobile app development platform in terms of output quality and whether they are willing to stick with this platform under formal (i.e., output and process) and informal (i.e., self-) control. We demonstrate that self-control has consistently stronger effects on application quality and platform stickiness than formal control modes. We also shed light on perceived autonomy as explanatory mechanism through which the control modes' effects are mediated. Taken together, our study highlights the theoretically important finding that self-determination among third-party developers is a stronger driving force than typical hierarchical control mechanisms. Implications for research and practice are discussed.

Keywords: Software-based platforms, Control mechanisms, Formal and self-control, Perceived autonomy, Mobile application quality, Platform stickiness

---

[1] The article is based on a preceding conference article (Goldbach and Kemper 2014) and was revised and extended to provide novel contributions above and beyond this previous article.

3.1 Introduction

Platform-based software ecosystems have dramatically changed the software industry in the way how software is developed, distributed and managed. In recent years, platforms such as Apple's App Store or Facebook's App Center have experienced a massive growth in terms of third-party developers, offered applications (apps) and overall revenues. Apple, for example, has reported six million registered app developers, more than one million active apps and revenues of 10 billion dollars from their App Store sales in 2013 (Apple 2014; Macstories 2013). Facebook recently announced that more than nine million apps are available on its social network contributed by more than two million third-party developers (Techcrunch 2011). A software platform is a software-based product or service that serves as a foundation on which outside parties can build complementary products or services and is defined as "*the extensible codebase of a software-based system that provides core functionality shared by the modules that interoperate with it and the interfaces through which they interoperate*" (Tiwana et al. 2010). The ecosystem surrounding such platforms includes numerous participants, namely the platform owner, third-party developers and platform users who are typically mutually dependent on one another.

The utility of almost any platform is increasingly shaped by the ecosystem that surrounds it. Take for example Apple's record-breaking iOS platform that includes the iPhone, iPod, and iPad. Its value to its myriads of users comes largely from over 1 million complementary apps over which Apple has little ownership. Compared to traditional software development settings, platforms utilize competences of independent and diverse third-party developers and therefore build on skills and innovative capacities which exceed the platform owners own capabilities. (Ceccagnoli et al. 2012). One of the platforms' goals is therefore to successfully leverage such new capabilities and innovations beyond the initial offered products and services. For a software-based platform to flourish, a large base of actively engaged and loyal third-party developers that produce high-quality applications is indispensable (Hartigh et al. 2006). Iansiti and Levien (2004b) for example found that productivity, robustness and niche creation are crucial performance indicators of ecosystem health which are in turn strongly driven by an active developer base that not only produces high-quality applications but also remains loyal to the platform ecosystem. Constantly attracting new developers and keeping them on their platforms while ensuring high output quality are thus important goals for the platform's long-term viability and success. Failing to constantly leverage third-party developers as a source of innovation may otherwise lead to negative consequences, as can be witnessed by the demise of several once-dominant platform protagonists such as Nokia or Blackberry that missed—among other problems—to create and manage a persistent pipeline of high-quality apps (Tiwana 2014). Given the need to maintain a prosperous platform ecosystem, the question arises of how to balance platform owners' objectives and strategies with third-party developers' behaviors and goals.

Traditional software development contexts are typically shaped by principal-agent relationships, where a principal delegates tasks to an agent who fulfils these tasks upon predefined contracts (Jensen and Meckling 1976). Because of incongruent goals and room for opportunistic behavior, the principal usually applies different formal control mechanisms (e.g., output or process control) to make the agents' activities or performance more transparent (Ouchi 1979). Software-based platforms, however, are distinct from traditional software development contexts for several reasons: First, the interests and goals of participants in platform ecosystems are not necessarily incongruent (Yoffie and Kwak 2006). Shared goals may for example be to produce high-quality apps to increase the platform's installed customer base and to generate revenues (Bergvall-Kåreborn et al. 2010; Tiwana 2014). Second, the relationship between a platform owner and third-party developers is typically less hierarchical and less compulsory. One major reason is that the huge number of mostly self-employed freelancers and hobbyists makes it prohibitively costly and time-consuming for platform owners to exercise tight control on each software app project (Klarner et al. 2013). More importantly, however, is the fact that developers can predominantly make their own decisions on platforms in terms of their activities, project requirements and products (Tiwana 2014) and therefore are more independent and enjoy a higher autonomy than in traditional software development contexts. Nevertheless, control modes are a substantial part of platform governance and different forms are implemented on actual platforms (Tiwana et al. 2010). Hence, this raises the question whether traditional formal control can be exercised in a platform context equally and with similar effects, or whether faciliating informal control leads to more promising results for software-based platforms.

In the IS domain, control modes have been extensively examined in internal as well as in outsourced and open-source IT projects to study, for example, the dynamics of control modes in IT projects (Kirsch 2004), their differential effects on team performance (Henderson and Lee 1992), or the balancing of control models in IS development offshoring projects (Gregory et al. 2013). However, there is as yet little understanding about the differential effects of control modes in software platform contexts, particularly with regard to a comparison of formal and self-control mechanisms and their effects on both work-related (i.e., work effort and output quality) and platform-related (i.e., loyalty to or stickiness with a platform) developer outcomes, even though several scholars have called for investigating such theoretically underexplored distinctions (e.g., Tiwana et al. 2013; Wareham et al. 2014). Moreover, previous research has largely focused on the nature and conditions of appropriate control modes in different contexts rather than on the differential effects of such modes on key developer performance outcomes (Tiwana and Keil 2009). In the few cases in which the effects of control modes have been investigated (e.g., Keil et al. 2013), the explanatory mechanism of *why* control modes influence developer performance outcomes remained largely implicit. Given the aforementioned importance of third-party developers' independence on software-based platforms, shedding light on the role of autonomy in explaining the relationship between platform control and developer behaviors may thus be helpful in opening this black box. The objective of this paper is therefore to address these gaps, guided by the following research questions:

(1) Which mode of platform control—formal control by the platform owner or self-control by third-party developers—leads to better outcomes in terms of development effort, app quality and platform stickiness?

(2) What is the role of third-party developers' perceived autonomy in the relationship between platform control modes and these outcomes?

Our study offers three noteworthy contributions to both research and practice. First, it contributes to the body of knowledge in the IS control literature—which is widely advanced in organizational and project-related contexts but relatively limited for software-based platforms (e.g., Tiwana et al. 2010)—by examining the differential effects of control modes on app developers' intentional and actual behaviors. Second, our study significantly adds to IS control research by identifying perceived autonomy as a critical explanatory mechanism through which control modes impact developers' platform- and work-related decisions, which goes beyond previous empirical studies that treated the relationship between control modes and performance outcomes largely as a black box (e.g., Keil et al. 2013). Third, by examining which and how control modes affect app developers' platform- and work-related decisions on software-based platforms, this study provides platform owners with valuable insights about the critical role of developers' autonomy in affecting their performance and loyalty, which speaks in favor of embracing soft power instruments (e.g., Yoffie and Kwak 2006) on software platforms to foster cooperation.

3.2 Theoretical Background

3.2.1 Platform Governance and Control Modes

One of the main challenges for software platform owners is to align their own objectives and strategies with the developer's activities and goals. This corresponds with the view of Tiwana et al. (2010) who see the central governance challenge for platform owners in finding the balance between retaining control to guarantee the platform's integrity and relinquishing control to foster developers' innovative capacity. Tiwana (2010) defines governance of a platform from a decision-making perspective including the partitioning of decision rights, the allocation of the ownership of the platform and its corresponding modules and, in particular, platform control. In this study, we focus on the latter governance mechanism.

According to control literature (Kirsch 1997; Ouchi 1979), control refers to a controller's attempts by which he or she influences an individual or an individual group (the controlee) to act in accordance with the objectives of the controller. Control is exercised with specific mechanisms, such as rules, regulations and incentives, which, when adopted by the controlee, result in activities and outcomes that are in line with the controller's objectives and goals. Control targets can be formulated and implemented in many forms with diverse approaches. As per control theory, two main categories of control mechanisms are typically distinguished, which are formal control and informal control modes. Formal control, on the one hand, is divided into output and process (or also called behavior) control. In terms of output control, controllers pre-specify output requirements and performance targets as objectives, which are then monitored, evaluated and accordingly rewarded. However, the specific actions to reach these objectives can be arbitrarily chosen by the controlee. By contrast, under process control, no specific outcomes are pre-determined and therefore free to be chosen by the controlee. Instead, specific procedures and methodologies are pre-defined and have to be followed by the controlee (i.e., are mandatory). For both types of formal control, evaluation information is required from the controlee, particularly on intermediate or final outputs (e.g., deliverables at predetermined milestones) or about controlees' adherence to the methods and procedures prescribed by the controller (Kirsch 1996).

On the other hand, informal control can be categorized into clan control and self-control (Ouchi 1979). In clan control, members of a group of controlees commit themselves to mutual goals and are monitoring, evaluating and correcting each other in accordance with their goals and their shared norms and values. Thus, the group members tend to adopt comparable processes and to produce outcomes with similar performance and quality. Under self-control, the individual controlees specify their own goals, evaluate themselves and decide on rewards or punishments based on their own performance. Control is thus not exercised by a group of controlees, but lies in the hands of each single controlee. Currently, a wide variety of formal and informal control modes are observed in software-based platforms (Wareham et al. 2014). Given that third-party developers are most often independent from one another and do not organize themselves in clans, self-control is the prevailing informal control mechanism on software platforms, in particular on consumer-oriented platforms (Tiwana 2014). Owing to the practical relevance of these control modes in platform settings, we will subsequently focus on process, output and self-control modes.

Previous IS research on control modes can be categorized in three major research streams, studying control modes either within organizations in internal IT projects, at the interface between organizations in IT outsourcing/offshoring relationships, or in more open settings such as open-source or software platform contexts. Prior studies that examined control modes within organizations have for example looked at the antecedents and choice of different control modes in IT project settings (Kirsch 1996; Kirsch 2004; Kirsch et al. 2002; Nidumolu and Subramani 2003), the effects of formal control on software development innovation and team performance (Cardinal 2001; Henderson and Lee 1992), and the role of clan control in IT projects (Chua et al. 2012). IS control research that shed light on inter-organizational settings has, for example, investigated the effectiveness of control modes in internal and outsourced projects (Tiwana and Keil 2009), the configuration of control portfolios in IT outsourcing and offshoring projects (Choudhury and Sabherwal 2003; Gregory et al. 2013; Rustagi et al. 2008; Srivastava and Teo 2012; Tiwana and Keil 2007) and relationship between formal and informal control in outsourced projects (Tiwana 2010). Control research on open-source projects has mainly focused on how control can be leveraged to influence developers' motivations and behaviors (e.g., Roberts et al. 2006). More recent studies have started to examine control also in platform ecosystem settings (e.g., McKnight et al. 2002). Ghazawneh and Henfridsson (2013), for example, have looked at the relationship between control and boundary resources on Apple's iPhone platform, whereas Wareham et al. (2014) investigated the tension between control and autonomy in a business software ecosystem. While all of the mentioned studies have laid the groundwork for understanding the nature, antecedents and conditions of control modes in traditional contexts, research on the differential effects of such control modes on software platforms has remained scarce. Moreover, previous studies have treated the impacts of control modes on performance outcomes largely as a black box without explicating why such effects are at work, thus leaving fundamental questions about control modes' effect mechanisms unanswered.

Taken together, although control mechanisms have been widely studied in IS research, there is still little understanding about *how* and *why different* control modes affect controlees' (i.e., third-party developers') behaviors and work outcomes in *software-based platforms*. Given the importance of third-party developers' independence on software-based platforms, we now cast light on the role of autonomy for developers' motivations to engage in, contribute to and stay with a platform, before we further elaborate on developer behaviors and performance outcomes that are crucial for software platforms.

3.2.2 Developer Autonomy on Software Platforms

As noted earlier, unlike traditional software development, the relationship between a platform owner and third-party developers is less hierarchical and less binding on software platforms, with only limited power of the platform owner to direct and instruct third-party developers. Formal individual contracts with detailed sanction mechanisms and requirements on how developers have to fulfil their work are thus less dominant. Hence, developers enjoy more freedom in determining their goals, project requirements and activities (Tiwana and Keil 2009). In addition, because of the huge amount of third-party developers, it is prohibitively costly for platform owners to exercise tight control on developers' activities and outputs. As such, developer's autonomy becomes a critical lever for the overall success of a software platform.

Self-determination theory provides a psychological framework for understanding the role of autonomy for individuals' intrinsic motivations (Deci and Ryan 2002). Autonomy refers to *"the degree to which a job provides substantial freedom, independence, and discretion to the individual in scheduling the work and in determining the procedures to be used in carrying it out"* (Hackman and Oldham 1976) and strongly builds on the principles of self-governance and self-regulation highlighting the importance of free will and choice when deciding on work procedures and outcomes. According to self-determination theory, it is particularly individuals' experience of autonomy that promotes intrinsic motivation for activities that lead to outcomes such as enhanced performance, quality, persistence, and creativity. Studies drawing on self-determination theory also found that autonomy is associated with higher intrinsic motivations, more creativity, higher self-esteem, less tensions and higher job satisfaction (Deci and Ryan 2002).

Self-determination and autonomy have been shown to play a crucial role in the empowerment of individuals, especially in work settings, that positively affect their work performance. According to Fernandez and Moldogaziev (2012), empowerment can be understood as a management strategy to share authority, resources, information and rewards with employees in order to make them feel more powerful. Two effects of empowerment are commonly distinguished in research literature that lend themselves to be applied to a software platform context: First, empowerments' direct effects refer to *work-related outcomes* encompassing individuals' effort and productivity (i.e., how hard they work) and employee's willingness to find newer and better ways to work, resulting in high-quality outcomes (i.e., how smart they work). Second, empowerments' indirect effects are associated with *job-related* outcomes that refer to individuals' more general perceptions of job satisfaction as well as trust in and loyalty towards their employer. Motivated to study third-party developer behaviors and performance outcomes on software platforms under formal and self-control modes, we adapt empowerment's distinction of direct and indirect effects to our research context by focusing on both *work-related* (i.e., application quality and development effort) and *platform-related outcomes* (i.e., developers' willingness to stick with a platform).

3.2.3 Developer Behaviors and Performance Outcomes on Software Platforms

Work-Related Outcomes: Application Quality and Development Effort
Two major work-related performance outcomes of third-party developers on software platforms are the effort they put into their work (input) and the resulting quality of the developed applications (output).

Effort is defined as the amount of energy and time a developer devotes to his development tasks relative to other developers. This conceptualization of effort is in line with previous organizational research wherein effort is characterized by the force, energy and activities which they put into their work (Churchill et al. 1985). Further, effort is also seen as part of work engagement that encompasses both individuals' willingness to work (i.e., their involvement and dedication) and their capability to work (i.e., their effort and vigor) to accomplish a task. High development effort on a platform is, for example, manifested in how often apps are released, updated and improved. Strong efforts on third-party developers' side are thus highly likely to strengthen a platform ecosystem in terms of its productivity, persistence and growth.

According to IS and website quality research (e.g., Gefen et al. 2003; Loiacono et al. 2007), the quality of applications refers to users' evaluations of an application's functionality, usefulness, ease of use and design. That is, when judging the quality of an application, users usually draw on different system indicators—related to a system's purpose, behaviors, accessibility and aesthetics—that together form the perception of the system's overall quality. In the context of software platforms, application quality is a particularly critical performance indicator of software platforms because the end-user market usually rewards high-quality output with strong sales and penalizes low-quality output with poor sales (Tiwana 2014). High-quality applications usually attract the lion's share of user attention, while poor quality applications most often disappear in the long tail of a platform's distribution of provided applications (e.g., Ghose et al. 2012). Consequently, a constant supply of high-quality applications contribute to an ecosystem's health through promoting positive self-reinforcing network effects that foster fast innovation cycles and strong user growth, while an overabundance of poor quality applications may even jeopardize a platform's survival.

Platform-Related Outcome: Platform Stickiness
As a crucial platform-related outcome, third-party developers' willingness to constantly participate in and stick with a platform over time has also been shown to maintain a healthy platform ecosystem (Ceccagnoli et al. 2012; Wareham et al. 2014). Accordingly, platform stickiness is a crucial performance factor that indicates a persistent relationship between a platform and its developers. Based on Zott et al. (2000), we define platform stickiness as the

ability of a platform to retain third-party developers on their platform, which is reflected in developers' intentions to continue contributing to a platform ecosystem. When developers continue to develop and update apps for the platform and to engage themselves in the platform community, they usually contribute to the platform's productivity, robustness and innovative capacity (Iansiti and Levien 2004b). By contrast, when developers switch to a rival platform, they are likely to destabilize the abandoned platform ecosystem through the drain of knowledge and expertise. Even worse, rival platforms and their customer bases may benefit from the influx of developers and their apps, which may ultimately overturn network and evolutionary effects in favor of rival platforms.

3.3 Hypotheses Development

In this section, we develop the theoretical rationale for our research model shown in Figure 3-1. We first present the hypotheses related to the differential effects of control modes on third-party developers' perceived autonomy, and on their work- and platform-related performance outcomes to address the question of *whether* and *which* control modes favorably affect developers' perceptions, behaviors and performance outcomes. This is followed by hypotheses related to the mediating role of perceived autonomy that may explain *how* and *why* control modes may affect such developer outcomes. Finally, we hypothesize the relationship between development effort and output (i.e., app) quality.

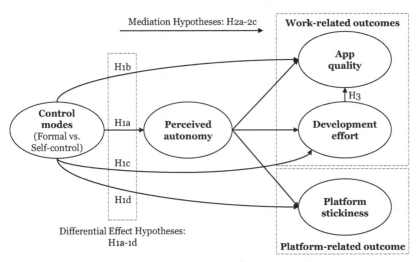

Figure 3-1: Research Model

3.3.1 Differential Effect Hypotheses

As mentioned before, formal control mechanisms are used by a controller to pre-specify either *what* the controlee should accomplish in a certain project (output control) or *how* the controlee should accomplish the project's objectives (process control). In contrast, self-control builds on self-regulation mechanisms and leaves much of the control work to the controlee. Based on this distinction of how control modes empower or constrain controlees in a given working relationship on software platforms, we argue that self-control will—all else being equal—lead (1) to higher perceived autonomy, (2) stronger work-related performance outcomes (i.e., more effort and higher application quality), and (3) higher platform stickiness than formal control, which will be theoretically developed next.

According to self-determination theory, an essential feature of autonomy is individuals' freedom to set their own goals and to work according to their own plans (Deci and Ryan 1987). In this regard, human beings' perceptions of autonomy have been found to be related to higher intrinsic motivation, less tension and higher work satisfaction (Deci and Ryan 2002; Pearce et al. 2003). That being said, any infringements on individuals' goals and endeavors from outside may thus reduce their autonomy and satisfaction with their work. Applied to the software platform context, we argue that compared to formal control modes, self-control modes will create a working environment that will be more favorable in supporting third-party developers' desire to work autonomously in the pursuit of their self-interests. This is mainly because self-control modes help developers strengthen their intrinsic motivations and thus self-regulatory behaviors to contribute apps to a platform, whereas formal control modes rather act as externally imposed requirements that are likely to hamper developers from perceiving and exercising autonomy in their daily work. Based on self-determination theory, we thus hypothesize that:

H1a: All else being equal, third-party developers will perceive higher autonomy under self-control than under formal control.

Under formal control conditions, controlees have to comply with pre-specified behaviors and/or outcomes. Controlees are urged to regularly verify and align their current activities and preliminary results with the given requirements. This may result in distractions and a lower awareness for their work procedures and outcomes. Even worse, pre-specified and tightly regulated work is often likely to result in an unenthusiastic, purely compliant response that produces inertia rather than pro-active endeavors (Ouchi 1979). In this regard, formal control often creates the impression of dependent controlees who are not able to achieve the best results on their own. This may also increase the need for closer supervision leading to even more compliant behaviors. As a result, tight controls usually stifle controlees' creativity and often interfere with their capabilities to reflect on their own activities and decisions (Amabile 1998; Orlikowski 1991), so that they are less able to find better ways in doing their jobs, resulting in less creative and more compliant work outcomes. In contrast, given the absence of pre-specified instructions on goals and procedures under self-control, controlees are able to be more reflective about their work and thus to think through their activities and goals. Moreover, they are more likely to perceive their outcomes as depending on their own efforts, initiatives and decisions, which naturally motivates them to invest more time and effort into their activities (Wang and Netemeyer 2002). Applying these arguments to the software platform context, we stipulate that in the pursuit of their vested self-interest, third-party developers will put more effort into their work practices and generate higher-quality applications under self-control than under formal control. This is largely because self-control modes create working conditions that are more in line with developers' personal goals and working practices. Accordingly, we hypothesize that:

H1b: All else being equal, third-party developers will produce higher quality apps under self-control than under formal control.

H1c: All else being equal, third-party developers will exert more effort in developing apps under self-control than under formal control.

The main steps to exercise formal control modes are in formulating the goals, and then monitoring, evaluating and correcting controlees' outcomes and processes according to these goals. In order to perform these steps, controllers heavily rely on evaluation information form controlees on intermediate and final outcomes (Kirsch 1996). From a control theoretical perspective, there is evidence that the exercise of such formal control modes with its evaluating and correcting activities is associated with feelings of oppression that reduce controlees' self-confidence and sense of belonging (Ouchi 1979). By contrast, self-control modes are by definition devoid of such infringements by the controller. Instead, given the enhanced degrees of freedom through self-regulation and the lack of tedious obligations, controlees are more likely to continue working even under negative experiences (Wang and Netemeyer 2002). These arguments suggest that third-party developers will have a higher tendency to keep contributing to and stick with a software platform's ecosystem (e.g., by submitting further apps or updates to platform) under self-control than under formal control.

H1d: All else being equal, third-party developers will have a higher intention to stick with a platform under self-control than under formal control.

3.3.2 Mediation Hypotheses

Given the high importance and prevalence of third-party developers' self-interest in platform ecosystems, we suggest that developers' perceived autonomy is one essential explanatory mechanism underlying the relationship between control modes and third-party developer behaviors.

Higher autonomy and self-guidance typically manifest themselves in a significantly higher intrinsic motivation of individuals to pursue tasks (Campbell and Pritchard 1976). Intrinsically motivated behaviors are usually considered more enjoyable, energizing and self-fulfilling than extrinsically motivated behaviors and often lead to greater persistence in increasing the quality of the behavior's and task's performance outcomes (Omodei and Wearing 1990). Furthermore, previous studies have shown that higher self-confidence evoked by higher autonomy positively affects the amount of effort employees invest into their work and into improving their performance outcomes (Bandura 1997). Employees are also more likely to focus longer on a task and to go the extra mile, when they feel autonomous and intrinsically motivated (Spreitzer 1995). Transferring these arguments to software platforms, we argue that developers' perceived autonomy plays a mediating role between control modes and developers' work-related outcomes. That is, when third-party developers work under self-control, they will *first* recognize and appreciate a more autonomous working environment that is characterized by self-regulation and self-directed decisions. This feeling of autonomy will *then* empower developers to put more effort into their activities and improve the quality of their outputs. Therefore, we propose that perceived autonomy will carry over the effects of control modes on developer effort and application quality. Put differently, we suggest that self-control, compared to formal control, will result in higher quality apps and higher developer effort *because* of higher perceived autonomy.

H2a: The effects of control modes on application quality are mediated by third-party developers' perceived autonomy.

H2b: The effects of control modes on third-party developers' effort in their work are mediated by developers' perceived autonomy.

As mentioned above, self-determination theory predicts that human beings' perceptions of autonomy are related to higher intrinsic motivation, more creativity, higher self-esteem, less tension and, ultimately, higher work satisfaction (Deci and Ryan 1987). Feelings of autonomy thus help people better realize their own goals, so that they are able to better identify themselves with the outcomes of their work. Any infringements upon individuals' endeavors from outside may reduce their autonomy and satisfaction with their work. Previous empirical research has also shown that employees feel more satisfied with their working place in an organization, when they are not under permanent scrutiny, but have greater leeway in developing and reaching their personal achievements (Hackman and Oldham 1976). Since third-party developers are less urged to deliver evaluation information to the platform and feel fewer infringements on their freedom to act independently under self-control than under formal control, they will perceive higher autonomy. This higher autonomy, in turn, is likely to translate into higher platform stickiness, given that developers feel more satisfied and comfortable with the platform under such circumstances. We thus suggest that perceived autonomy will mediate the relationship between control modes and platform stickiness. In other words, self-control will lead to higher platform stickiness than formal control *because* of higher perceived autonomy.

H2c: The effects of control modes on third-party developers' intention to stick with a platform are mediated by developers' perceived autonomy.

3.3.3 The Relationship between Development Effort and Application Quality

Previous research studies could demonstrate a positive association between work effort and output quality (e.g., Christen et al. 2006). When employees immerse themselves in a task and invest time and effort to probe different techniques and solutions, they usually come up with more creative and higher-quality outcomes than when they would spend less effort (Johnson et al. 2003). In line with that logic, we argue that third-party developers who put more effort into their work will produce higher-quality apps. Spending more effort into app development will likely result in more iterations to test and compare different functionalities and designs and will thus incrementally improve the application's overall quality. We therefore propose that:

H3: Third-party developer's effort in their work is positively associated with the quality of their apps.

3.4 Research Methodology

3.4.1 Experimental Design, Procedures and Treatments

We conducted a laboratory experiment based on a self-programmed mobile app mock-up development platform to test our hypotheses. We used electronic mail and posts on social networking websites to recruit subjects from a public university for our experiment in exchange for a small participation fee (5€). After arriving in our lab, participants were asked to take a seat in front of a computer and were given all information to understand the three parts of the experiment. The first part covered socio-demographic questions that were presented in a pre-experimental questionnaire. In the second part, before the subjects were assigned to one of the three experimental conditions (see Table 3-1), each subject was exposed to the same baseline set-up of our development platform which served as a benchmark based on adaptation theory (Helson 1964). In this way, participants were able to establish a common frame of reference ensuring that the context and background of their experimental experiences were homogeneous across conditions and the disparities across different conditions were caused only by our treatments.

Table 3-1: Experimental Design and Instructions

Informal control	Formal control ($n = 93$)	
Self-Control (n = 45)	Process Control ($n = 48$)	Output Control ($n = 45$)
• No guidelines • Self-organized work	• Implementation sequence for the task was pre-given • No output criteria for app mock-up were specified	• Specific output criteria for the app mock-up were pre-given • Implementation sequence was at the discretion of participant

After presenting the baseline platform (including a tutorial video), the subjects were randomly assigned to one of three experimental conditions and were instructed to step into the shoes of a platform developer to create a mobile app mock-up for a new mobile platform. More specifically, the developers' concrete mission was to design a hotel app for that platform with free-to-choose design and functionalities. As incentive, the subjects were informed that the best app mock-ups would be entered into a raffle where they could win a tablet PC. Based on results of a pre-test with 10 subjects, in which we varied the length of development time, participants were given 20 minutes to design the hotel app. A pop-up window regularly reminded the subjects about the remaining time. While the subjects designed their app mock-ups, we collected clickstream data including the number of clicks, the number of elements added to and removed from the mock-up screens. After 20 minutes, the subjects were forwarded to a post-experimental questionnaire. In this third part of the experiment, subjects were surveyed on questions regarding platform stickiness and perceived autonomy. We also included questions on manipulation checks in this survey. The average duration of the experimental sessions was 33.53 minutes ($SD = 3.37$).

In our experiment, we employed control modes (i.e., output, process and self-control) as treatments in a 3 (control modes) x 1 between-subjects design (see Table 1). In order to obtain experimental groups of approximately the same size, we implemented a blocked randomization process (Kirk 2012). Participants were assigned to a group according to randomly permuted lists of the three groups. In the process control mode, and consistent with previous studies (Kirsch 1996), participants were required to follow a specific sequence of tasks to create their mobile app mock-up. However, no specific output criteria (e.g., about the final design and appearance of the mock-up) had to be fulfilled. For example, subjects first should choose the background color of the app, and then write a title, and the like. In contrast, participants in the output control condition were indicated to fulfill specific output criteria (e.g., about the design and layout of the app). In this control mode, however, the sequence of implementing these output standards was not pre-given but could be freely chosen by the participants. As an example, the apps should have a bluish background or navigation buttons on the bottom of the app screens. In the self-control condition, participants received no specific prescriptions but were rather instructed to organize themselves when creating the app mock-ups on the development platform. Based on the above mentioned pre-test with 10 subjects, we refined the wording of the instructions and fine-tuned the experimental procedure.

Figure 3-2 depicts a screenshot of the self-programmed mobile app mock-up development platform. While the experimental instructions were presented at the left of the website, the screens of the smartphone apps that had to be designed were displayed in the center. Elements for the app could be filled in via drag-and-drop by using app elements from a design kit at the right hand side. Typical design elements were background styles, text fields, buttons, a selection of icons and images as well as specific mobile elements. Inserted elements could be further modified by changing the color, style and size of the elements.

Figure 3-2: Experimental Mobile App Development Platform with Instructions (Left Panel), Working Space (Middle Panel), and Design Kit (Right Panel)

3.4.2 Subjects

145 students from a large public university in Germany participated in our controlled laboratory experiment. Seven cases had to be dropped from the sample because of the following reasons: two participants had technical problems and failed to complete the second

part of the questionnaire. Five participants were dropped because of inconsistencies in their responses. Our final sample thus contained 138 participants with an average age of 22.6 ($SD = 4.5$) years. 83 percent were male. The majority of participants (i.e., 90 %) had a technical background studying computer science, business informatics, or business engineering. Furthermore, about 75 % ($n = 106$) of the participants reported that they had previous experience in software development, app development, prototyping or computer aided design.

3.4.3 Measurement Characteristics

Measures for platform stickiness were adapted from the website stickiness construct of Li et al. (2006) and adjusted to the platform context. Participants' perceived autonomy was measured using a single-item derived from self-determination literature (Deci and Ryan 2002) and based on findings that the predictive validity of single items is comparable to multi-item measures (e.g., Mayer et al. 1995; Sarstedt and Wilczynski 2009). Subjects' effort during their app mock-up development activities were measured using subjects' objective clickstream data collected during the experiment. We measured developer effort by averaging the number of elements added to and removed from the app mock-up during the experiment because this reflected the intensity and engagement with which the subjects developed and refined their app mock-up. We also collected control variables (i.e., age, gender, possession and usage of smartphone, subjects' general profit-making orientation, experiences in prototyping and computer aided design, and in software and app development) and included manipulation checks. All items of the study's constructs and their sources are shown in Table 3-2.

Table 3-2: Measurement Items

Constructs	Indicators	Source
Perceived Autonomy	While designing the app, I was autonomous to decide on my course of actions.	Adapted from Deci and Ryan (2002)
Platform stickiness	If available, I would expect my use of such a platform including similar instructions to continue in the future.	Adapted from Dahui et al. (2006)
	If available, I would intend to continue using such a platform including similar instructions in the future.	
	If available, I would plan to keep using such a platform including similar instructions in the future.	
Manipulation checks	The instructions on the app development platform indicated me to	Developed by the authors, based on Benlian and Hess (2007)
	...follow a specific sequence of tasks/steps to create the app.	
	... fulfill specific output criteria regarding the app's design.	

Note: All items measured with 5-point Likert scales, anchored at (1) strongly disagree and (5) strongly agree

3.4.4 Post-Hoc Assessment: Expert Ratings of Mobile App Quality

To evaluate the quality of the 138 app mock-ups designed by the subjects, we created a web-based survey for an expert rating. In the survey, the app mock-up screens were displayed together with a 6-point rating scale (anchored at (1) = strongly disagree to (6) = strongly agree). We measured quality of the app mock-up with a single-item ("The app-mockup has a high overall quality") adapted from Wells et al. (2011) based on the notion to capture an overall perception of app quality and not specific facets of it. Given the high number of app mock-ups that had to be evaluated, a one item assessment was an acceptable compromise to balance expert rating efforts with measurement accuracy. Previous studies comparing single-item and multiple-item measures could show that the predictive validity of single items is comparable to multi-item measures (e.g., Mayer et al. 1995; Sarstedt and Wilczynski 2009), in particular, when the rating object (in our case the app) and the rating attribute (in our case app quality) are sufficiently concrete (e.g., when raters are supported through a visual display of the objects to be rated and receive a common definition of the rating attribute). Five experts (i.e., two IS academics with a research focus in app development and three IS practitioners with long experience in the mobile business) were invited to conduct the expert ratings from a customer's point of view. In order to obtain a common baseline understanding of the mock-ups' quality, the experts were shown 20 mock-ups in a random order before they could start with their ratings, and the meaning of app quality was defined and clarified based on examples. Then, the experts were asked to assess the quality of the 138 app mock-ups that were presented randomly to each rater. The inter-rater reliability among the five experts resulted in a Cronbach's alpha $\alpha = .85$ indicating high consistency between the raters (e.g., Krippendorff 2004). We thus used these ratings as measurement items for app quality in our data analysis.

3.5 Results

3.5.1 Manipulation Checks and Control Variables

To confirm the random assignment of subjects to the different experimental conditions, we performed several one-way ANOVAs. There were no significant differences in gender ($F = 0.01$, $p > .1$), age ($F = 0.57, p > .1$), possession of a smartphone ($F = 2.77$, $p > .05$), usage of a smartphone ($F = 0.93$, $p > .1$), subjects' general profit-making orientation ($F = 0.89$, $p > .05$), experience in software development ($F = 1.31, p > .1$), experience in app development ($F = 0.17$, $p > .1$), experience in computer-aided design prototyping ($F = 1.35$, $p > .1$), and experience in image processing ($F = 1.13$, $p > .1$) among the experimental conditions. These results indicate that participants' characteristics and experience were not the cause of the differences in their perceptions and intentions. To check the manipulation of the different types of experimental conditions, we ran a MANOVA. We found a significant overall effect of the MANOVA ($\lambda = .72$, F [4,133] = 13.24, $p < .001$). Subjects in the formal control conditions indicated that they perceived significantly higher levels of (external) control than subjects in the self-control treatment. In summary, these results indicate that the treatments were successfully executed.

3.5.2 Comparison of Control Mechanisms' Differential Effects

A MANOVA test was conducted to test the differential effects of the control mechanisms. MANOVA test statistics included Pillari's trace, Wilks' lambda, Hotelling's trace, and Roy's largest root. The p-values of these statistics were found to be significant ($p < .05$). Therefore, further ANOVAs were conducted on the four dependent variables. The subsequent ANOVA tests (see Table 3-3) revealed a significantly higher platform stickiness in the self-control condition than in the formal control condition ($F = 8.02$, $p < .05$). Similarly, perceived autonomy was rated significantly higher in the self-control condition than in the formal control condition ($F = 9.43$, $p < .01$). We found similar results for the expert ratings of app quality. Experts rated those app mock-ups significantly higher regarding app quality that were developed in the self-control condition compared to those created in the formal control condition ($F = 8.40$, $p < .01$). In contrast to the findings above, we could not find any significant differences between the experimental conditions in terms of developer effort ($F = .23$, $p > .05$). Based on these results, H1a, H1b and H1d could be supported, while H1c had to be rejected. We made qualitatively similar findings when we compared the four dependent variables between the output, process and self-control conditions individually.

Table 3-3: ANOVA Results and Group Means (SD) for Self-Control vs. Formal Control Conditions

	Self-control (n = 45)	Formal control (n = 93)	ANOVA		
	M (SD)	M (SD)	Df	F	p
App Quality	3.62 (.74)	3.11 (1.00)	1	8.40	.004
Effort	19.09 (5.20)	18.63 (5.32)	1	.23	.635
Platform stickiness	3.53 (.95)	3.05 (.90)	1	8.02	.005
Perceived autonomy	3.91 (.93)	3.34 (1.06)	1	9.43	.003

3.5.3 Test of the Research Model

For testing mediation and the fit of the theoretical model with the data, we used structural equation modeling (SEM) package Mplus 5.2 (Muthén and Muthén 2010) with maximum likelihood estimation and bootstrapping (95% bootstrap confidence interval (CI)). The advantage of SEM over regression analysis is the simultaneous consideration of several dependent variables in one unified model and the inclusion of error terms on the measurement item level.

Measurement Model Assessment

The psychometric properties of the measurement models were assessed by examining individual item loadings, internal consistency, convergent validity, and discriminant validity of all latent constructs. Convergent validity for latent constructs was evaluated using three criteria recommended by Fornell and Larcker (1981): (1) all measurement factor loadings must be significant and above the threshold value of .70, (2) the composite reliabilities should exceed .80, and (3) the average variance extracted (AVE) by each construct must exceed the variance due to measurement error for that construct (i.e., AVE should exceed 0.50). All loadings of the measurement items on their respective factors were all significant ($p < 0.05$) and above the recommended threshold values (Chin and Todd 1995). Composite reliabilities of the constructs were $\alpha = .89$ for platform stickiness, and $\alpha = .87$ for app quality. The values for AVEs were .74 for platform stickiness, and .56 for app quality. Thus, these constructs met the norms for convergent validity. In addition, for satisfactory discriminant validity, the square root of the AVE from the construct should be greater than the variance shared between a construct and other constructs in the model (Fornell and Larcker 1981). All of the square roots of the AVE also exceeded the corresponding inter-construct correlations, providing strong evidence of discriminant validity. Hence, the latent constructs in this study represent concepts that are both theoretically and empirically distinguishable.

Structural Model Analysis

Results from the theoretical model analysis show a nonsignificant χ^2 statistic of 53.80 ($p > .05$, $df = 39$). Fit indices indicate an adequate fit with CFI = .98, RMSEA = .052 and SRMR = .049. Overall, these results indicate a good fit of the theoretical model with the data (e.g., Hu and Bentler 1999). Results of the model are shown in Figure 3-3 including path coefficients and the variance explained (R^2 values). The model successfully explained a considerable portion of variance in app quality ($R^2 = 0.39$), and platform stickiness ($R^2 = 0.22$), while explaining just a low amount of variance in perceived autonomy ($R^2 = 0.07$) and development effort ($R^2 = 0.04$). When leaving perceived autonomy out of the model (i.e., our mediating variable), the results were consistent with our ANOVA findings. While there were positive and significant effects of control modes on app quality and platform stickiness (both $p < .05$), we could not identify a significant effect of control modes on development effort ($\beta = -.05$; $p > .01$). However, in support of H3, we found a positive significant effect of effort on app quality ($\beta = .43, p < .001$).

Our mediation hypotheses were assessed based on bootstrapping procedures recommended by Preacher and Hayes (2008). In addition to a positive significant direct effect of control modes on app quality ($\beta = .24$, $p < .01$) after introducing perceived autonomy into our model, we found a significant indirect effect of control modes on app quality via perceived autonomy

($\beta = .07$, $p < .05$). Perceived autonomy thus significantly and partially mediated the relationship between control modes and app quality, in support of H2a. Furthermore, we found a significant and fully mediated indirect effect ($\beta = .11$, $p < .01$) from control modes to platform stickiness via perceived autonomy (i.e., the direct effect of control modes on platform stickiness became non-significant), supporting H2c. Finally, we found no significant indirect effects from control modes to development effort ($\beta = .05$, $p > .05$). Thus, H2b could not be supported.

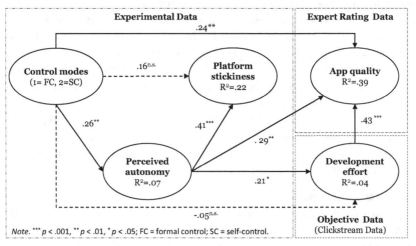

Figure 3-3: Results of SEM Analysis

3.6 Discussion

The main objective of this study was to investigate *whether* and *why* formal control and self-control exert differential effects on developers' work- and platform-related outcomes in platform ecosystems. Three key findings can be derived from our study. First, our findings show that, all else being equal, self-control is superior to formal control in strengthening developers' platform stickiness, while simultaneously ensuring higher application quality. Conversely, third-party developers exposed to formal control are less likely to contribute high-quality apps to a platform, yet are more likely to churn to rival Second, our study shows that developers' perceived autonomy serves as an important mediator between control mechanisms and crucial developer performance outcomes. More specifically, and because we found evidence for significant mediation mechanisms, perceived autonomy provides a central explanatory argument for *why* self-control is superior to formal control in increasing platform stickiness and application quality—it is superior *because* third-party developers perceive significantly higher autonomy under self-control than under formal control.

Third, while we could not show that formal and self-control were differentially related to developers' work efforts, perceived autonomy was found to significantly affect development efforts that, in turn, had a strong influence on app quality. These findings lead to interesting implications.

3.6.1 Implication for theory and practice

From a theoretical standpoint, this study offers a deeper understanding of the effect mechanisms relating control modes on software platforms with developers' work- and platform-related outcomes. We show in our study that it is self-control—and not formal control—that is more conducive in platform ecosystems to both developers' subjective perceptions (i.e., platform stickiness) and objective behavioral outcomes (i.e., application quality). This is all the more important to understand because platform ecosystems cannot exist or prosper without the contributions of highly motivated developers who are willing and able to continuously contribute high-quality applications. Previous studies of control effects in IS development have only scarcely considered whether control modes differentially relate to developer performance outcomes. However, it is important to understand whether all types of control modes affect developer behaviors equally or in the same way, because some control modes may strongly affect developer performance whereas others may not be as salient. Based on our study findings, the emergence of platform ecosystems obviously makes some types of control more prominent than others. Our study is, to the best of our knowledge, the first to establish the heightened importance of self-control and perceived autonomy as intrinsic motivational drivers for developers' stickiness with and high-quality work on a software platform. It thus contributes to IS control literature by studying control mechanisms in a yet underexplored context and advances platform governance literature by highlighting the shifting balance between formal and informal control mechanisms on software platforms. More broadly, our study's findings point towards a more balanced and less hierarchical power relationship between platform owners and developers and away from traditional principal-agent relationships.

A second contribution of this study relates to the explanation of why control modes affect developers' behaviors and performance on software platforms. While previous control studies in IS research have treated the relationship between control modes and performance outcomes largely as a black box, our study identified perceived autonomy as a crucial explanatory mechanism through which control modes impact developers' behaviors and performance. This study thus contributes to an advanced understanding of *why* control modes differentially affect developers' behaviors and their performance outcomes.

Finally, contrary to beliefs that self-control mechanisms attract masses of third-party developers who produce just poor quality applications due to the lack of direction and integrity (e.g., Hagiu and Halaburda 2010), our study's findings show that self-control seems not only to increase stickiness compared to formal control, but also to facilitate that higher-quality applications are contributed to a platform. This finding underscores the importance of self-regulatory forces in directing developers' work and shows that, stated colloquially, letting a thousand flowers grow can be positive for the health of platform ecosystems (Boudreau 2012). Although we constrained our focus in this study to pure forms of control modes without considering control portfolios that could eventually have more favorable impacts, examining the distinct effects of self-control vs. formal control adds to existing IS control literature by providing a more nuanced understanding of single control modes' relative effectiveness.

Given that platforms gaining in importance as internet-based business models (Janowicz and Noorderhaven 2006), our results have also important implications for practice. First, in platform ecosystems, it is important to understand whether all types of control modes affect developer behaviors equally. Thus, for platform owners who are trying to attract and motivate developers to contribute to their platform or to sustain their level of participation, it is imperative to understand which types of control modes are likely to generate more (or less) developer participation and output (i.e., app) quality. Our study suggests that self-control mechanisms are superior to formal control modes in generating higher platform stickiness, while simultaneously motivating developers to deliver higher-quality apps. Platform owners may therefore benefit from this study by carefully testing and monitoring the relative effectiveness of different self-control mechanisms vis-à-vis formal control modes on their software platforms. Examples for such self-control mechanisms may include open access to developers' contribution and performance statistics or the availability of IT tools helping developers manage themselves and their work in a self-reliant way.

Second, our experimental findings underscore the need for platform owners to recognize and leverage developers' autonomy as a critical asset, because—as we found in our study—too much infringement on developers' plans and endeavors can undermine their willingness to stick with and contribute high-quality apps to a platform. Consequently, and consistent with previous recommendations (Claussen et al. 2013; Yoffie and Kwak 2006), we therefore suggest that in contrast to classical hard power instruments such as financial incentives or sanctions, platform owners should increasingly embrace more soft power instruments to bring developers onto a common path. Such soft power instruments may emphasize the use of intangible resources (e.g., private market intelligence or information about future plans) to build legitimacy and trust, and persuade developers to consider shared goals and a compelling platform vision.

3.6.2 Limitations, Future Research and Conclusion

As with any study, there are some limitations that provide opportunities for future research. First, based on our self-programmed mobile platform, we simulated an app development process and platform control mechanisms in a laboratory setting, which is rather artificial and thus limits the external validity of our study. Although our explicit focus of this study was on establishing a causal link between control modes and developer behaviors on a platform and thus on maximizing internal validity, future research is needed to verify our findings in a more realistic setting and with a longer-term focus. Second, to isolate the distinct effects of formal control vs. self-control modes, we treated these two control mechanisms as dichotomous, mutually exclusive phenomena. However, we are aware that in reality, a variety of different controls are simultaneously selected from both formal and informal options as part of control portfolios. A fruitful avenue for future research may thus be to study the complementary or substitutive effects of combining different control modes on developer behaviors on software platforms and how these effects vary over time. Third, our lab experiment was conducted drawing on university students as participants. Although we believe that the students participating in our study had technical backgrounds and skills very similar to our target population, one should be cautious to generalize our results to a real-life setting. Further research is encouraged to conduct lab and field studies with a more representative mix of third-party developers. Fourth, although we controlled for several important confounding factors (e.g., development experience, profit-making orientation), we acknowledge that there may be factors that could not be completely accounted for in our rather artificial lab experiment (e.g., multi-homing scenarios or the competitive intensity between developers). Future studies should include and control for these and other factors (e.g., specific intrinsic or extrinsic motives, trust and satisfaction) as alternative explanations for why and how well developers participate in a platform ecosystem. Finally, future work may extend our research model by including other developer-related outcome variables that are important for the success and prosperity of platform ecosystems and may be influenced by different control modes, such as developers' creativity or innovativeness and architectural choices.

To conclude, we believe that examining control mechanisms in software-based ecosystems is a rich avenue for future research, especially given that hitherto under-researched control modes such as self-control are gaining in importance. We hope this study gives fresh impetus to researchers to refine our understanding about third-party developers' behaviors on and contributions to software platforms.

Chapter 4: Informal Control and Intrinsic Motivation on Software Platforms

Title: Understanding Informal Control Modes on Software Platforms – The Mediating Role of Third-Party Developers' Intrinsic Motivation

Authors: Goldbach, Tobias, Technische Universität Darmstadt, Germany

Benlian, Alexander, Technische Universität Darmstadt, Germany

Published in: International Conference on Information Systems (ICIS 2015), December 13-16, 2015, Fort Worth, United States

Abstract

Software ecosystem platforms such as Google's Play Store or Apple's App Store rely heavily on highly motivated third-party developers who are eager to invest their time and effort into developing and updating apps for platforms. Platform owners are challenged to find a balance between developers' need for autonomy and a platform's integrity. Despite the widely acknowledged importance of informal control modes in such contexts, limited empirical work exists on how and why clan and self-control affect developers' behaviors and performance outcomes on software platforms. Drawing on control theory and motivation literature, we conducted an online survey with 230 Android developers to examine how developers' intrinsic motivation mediates the effects of informal control modes on developer performance. Our findings show that while intrinsic motivation plays an important role in mediating both informal control modes' effects, clan control exhibits predominantly stronger downstream effects than self-control. Implications for research and practice are discussed.

Keywords: Informal Control Modes, Intrinsic Motivation, Development Effort, Intention to Stay, Software Platforms

4.1 Introduction

Software platforms have offered novel ways for third-party developers to develop, manage and distribute software. By providing programming interfaces and developer tools, platform owners deliberately open their organization and enable external developers to extent the core functionality of the platform and to distribute applications via the platform marketplace (Boudreau 2012). In recent years, platform owners were able to build prospering and profitable ecosystems, such as Apple's App Store, Google's Play Store or the Facebook App Centre. In Q4 2014, Google's Play Store offered 1.43 million apps, published by nearly 400,000 developers. A total of $25 billion have been earned cumulatively by Apple developers from their app sales since 2008 (Apple 2015) and shipments of smartphones worldwide have grown by a 27.7% in 2014 to 1.3 billion (IDC 2015).

Platform owners build on third-party developers' competences and innovative capacities and thus focus on attracting, motivating and keeping developers on their platform (Ceccagnoli et al. 2012). By doing so, platforms are able to increase their output and innovation rates and to improve their reaction abilities regarding the needs of customers and the overall market (Boudreau and Lakhani 2009). Consequently, it is rational for platform owners to create an environment in which developers are continuously motivated to invest their time and effort for developing and improving their apps. From a platform governance view, platform owners are challenged to harmonize their own strategies with the developers' activities and goals (Tiwana et al. 2010). A diverse set of formal and informal control modes are typically exercised on platforms to motivate beneficial developer (i.e., controlee) behaviors (Tiwana et al. 2010). Given the large number of developers and development projects on software platforms, exercising tight control on each project becomes, however, tremendously costly and time-consuming. As a result, informal control modes (i.e., self-control and clan control), which rely on people skills and self-regulation, have been found to gain in importance in decentralized and complex multi-project settings such as software platforms (Goldbach et al. 2014; Kirsch 2004; Tiwana et al. 2013).

Two research gaps in the IS literature regarding control modes are particular noteworthy. First, studies have largely focused on understanding the nature, antecedents and choice of formal and informal control modes (e.g., Choudhury and Sabherwal 2003; Chua et al. 2012; Henderson and Lee 1992; Kirsch 1996; Kirsch 1997; Kirsch et al. 2010; Kirsch et al. 2002) and only a few studies have analyzed the downstream effects of control modes. Studies focused almost exclusively on effects of formal control modes, resulted in mixed findings regarding the effects of clan control, or did not provide an explanatory argument why an effect occurs (Gopal and Gosain 2010; Keil et al. 2013; Tiwana 2010; Tiwana and Keil 2009). Second, most IS control studies have either focused on internal projects (Cardinal 2001; Chua et al. 2012; Kirsch 1996; Kirsch 2004; Kirsch et al. 2010) or outsourced projects (Gregory et al. 2013; Rustagi et al. 2008; Srivastava and Teo 2012; Tiwana and Keil 2009). Studies in more open settings have analyzed the relationship between control and boundary resources on the Apple platform (Ghazawneh and Henfridsson 2013), or the relation between control and autonomy in a business technology ecosystem (Wareham et al. 2014).

Furthermore, motivation is well studied as an important factor influencing behaviors and performance (Locke and Latham 2004). Surprisingly, and to the best of our knowledge, there is limited research and empirical evidence on the relationship between different control modes and controlees' motivation. Intrinsic motivation, based on an individual's inherit interest in an activity, has been found to be superior to other forms of motivation (Carton 1996; Deci and Ryan 2000) and intrinsic motivation plays a predominate role in more open environments (Ke and Zhang 2009). Therefore, we further want to shed light on the link between informal control and developers' intrinsic motivation on software platforms.

In summary, our knowledge regarding the effects of informal control modes on third-party developers' behaviors and outcomes on software platforms is still limited and we lack a deeper understanding of how developers' intrinsic motivation drives these effects. In order to contribute to these research gaps, the purpose of our study is to analyze the effects of self-control and clan control on third-party developers' intrinsic motivation and the role of intrinsic motivation as a possible explanation for why and how informal control modes affect crucial developer outcomes and behaviors. Our study is guided by two research questions:

(1) *How does self-control and clan control affect third-party developers' intrinsic motivation.*

(2) *Does developers' intrinsic motivation mediate the relationship between informal control modes and crucial developer behaviors and outcomes?*

For answering these questions, we conducted an online survey with 230 Android developers. Our study provides several theoretical contributions by offering a deeper understanding on how informal control modes operate and positively influence third-party developer behaviors, outcomes and intentions on software platforms. We not only respond to several research calls on analyzing how informal control modes operate on software platforms (Tiwana et al. 2013; Wareham et al. 2014), but also provide empirical evidence for a mediating role of third-party developers' intrinsic motivation in the relationship between informal control modes and developers' effort and intention to stay on the platform. We are thus contributing particularly to IS control literature by providing an explanation of why informal control positively affects developer performance. Third, our study also provides practical insights for platform owners that high-quality performance outcomes can be achieved on software platforms by embracing more soft power instruments rather than exercising tight control.

Our paper is organized as follows: We first present the theoretical background of our study and develop our research model and hypotheses. We then describe our research methodology followed by our results. The paper concludes with a discussion of key findings, implications and directions for further research.

4.2 Theoretical Background

4.2.1 Platform Governance and Informal Control Modes

A platform owner usually strives to attain a healthy and viable platform ecosystem, which means durability and growth for the platform (Hartig et al. 2006). One goal of platform owners is to attract, motivate and keep third-party developers, in order to utilize their competences and skills for the platform (Ceccagnoli et al. 2012). According to Tiwana et al. (2010), platform governance can be defined as who makes what decision on and about a platform, including the allocation of decision rights, the ownership of a platform and its third-party modules, and lastly the control of behaviors and outcomes on a platform. Control refers to the controller's attempts to influence and motivate an individual or a group of individuals (the controlee) to act accordingly to the controller's objectives (Ouchi 1980).

Control mechanisms are typically divided into formal control and informal control modes (e.g., Kirsch 1997; Kirsch et al. 2002): On the one hand, formal control modes are divided into behavior control and outcome control. With output control, controllers pre-specify desirable output requirements and performance targets as objectives in advance, for example by written contracts, which are then monitored, evaluated and accordingly rewarded. By contrast, with behavior control, specific procedures and methodologies are pre-determined, while characteristics of outcomes are free to be chosen by the controlee (Kirsch et al. 2002). On the other hand, informal control modes build on social skills and meanings of self-regulation, based on shared norms and values of groups or individuals. Informal control refers to self-control and clan control. With self-control, individuals set their own goals, monitor themselves and sanction or reward themselves in accordance. Controllers may build an environment suitable for self-regulatory behaviors. By providing tools and trainings for self-regulation as well as information and statistics needed for making decisions, controlees are able to organize and evaluate themselves (Kirsch et al. 2002). Clan control enables controllers to reduce the differences between controlee's activities and their own strategies. By promulgating shared values, beliefs or common goals, controlees as members of a group typically commit themselves to these shared values and beliefs and therefore tend to adopt similar procedures and comparable performance outcomes. Clan control therefore helps to maintain the controlee's integrity without exercising tide control. Clan control is likely to lead to a sense of cohesiveness among clan members, which in turn facilitates self-regulatory mechanisms on a group level (e.g., evaluating and correcting each other) in accordance with shared values and beliefs (Kirsch et al. 2002). Shared values, norms and common goals are not only propagated by a controller but also emerge and are encouraged by members of an effective clan (Kirsch 1997; Turner and Makhija 2006). Self- and clan control are particularly important when outcomes are unclear or difficult to measure and behavior is hard to specify or not observable (Kirsch 1996; Kirsch et al. 2002; Kohli and Kettinger 2004).

Although control literature has a long tradition in IS research, recent studies have noted our limited knowledge about how different control modes operate and affect individuals, especially regarding third-party developers on highly dynamic and multi-project based software platform contexts (Ghazawneh and Henfridsson 2013; Goldbach et al. 2014; Tiwana et al. 2013; Wareham et al. 2014). In particular Tiwana et al. (2010) pointed out that control on software platforms requires a delicate balance between third-party developers' need for autonomy and a platform's integrity. They further noted that exercising strict formal control on every development project may become tremendously costly and time-consuming or even be redundant, given that interests among these two parties are not principally divergent. Against this backdrop, we believe that exercising informal control modes presents an opportunity to grant developers a certain amount of autonomy while simultaneously bringing developers onto a common path of shared values, beliefs and goals, without the need for tight supervision and regulation. This is in line with previous studies which stated that informal control and soft-power instruments are particular important in such decentralized and complex multi-project contexts (Kirsch 2004; Tiwana et al. 2010; Yoffie and Kwak 2006). However, there is still limited understanding on how and why informal control modes affect third-party developers' behaviors, outcomes and intentions on software-platforms. Previous research on the downstream effects of control modes have primarily focused on formal control modes in outsourcing contexts and the few studies that looked at the consequences of clan control showed only limited or inconclusive findings (Gopal and Gosain 2010; Keil et al. 2013; Tiwana 2010; Tiwana and Keil 2009).

A variety of formal and informal control mechanisms can be observed on software platforms (Tiwana 2014). Self-control manifests itself in different parts on the platform. While Apple, for example, tightly approves every app that is published on the platform in order to secure quality and the adherence of development guidelines, such an approval process is largely absent on Google's Android platform and therefore the responsibility lies within self-control of third-party developers. Moreover, ensuring that development projects finish within budget and schedule is typically overseen by third-party developers themselves (Bergvall-Kåreborn and Howcroft 2011). To interact with each other, third-party developers usually participate in platform-dedicated online communities (e.g., developer.apple.com or developer.android.com). Additional channels for sharing information, knowledge, expertise and best practice solutions are forums, wikis, blogs, chats and developer conferences. Platform owners typically establish and interact with developers in such communities and social media channels in order to create clan control on software platforms. As an example, Apple products are promoted as being well designed and innovative as well as implying a trendy lifestyle, which in turn is shown in the design, usability and user experience of the products, reflecting the Apple brand. Android, on the other side, is a more open and less regulated platform and Android developers aim at a wide variety of devices, diversity in offered apps and customizability for customers (Bergvall-Kåreborn and Howcroft 2011). App developers mainly share such norms and values, which in turn is manifested in their development approaches, functionalities and design of third-party apps. Common norms and goals in a development context may also be the adherence to coding and design standards, naming conventions, testing processes and framework usage. The exercise of control mechanisms may vary across different platforms (mobile, social media, open source). However, this study focuses on mobile platforms.

4.2.2 Third-Party Developers Intrinsic Motivation

As mentioned earlier, control is defined as controller's attempts to influence and motivate an individual or a group to act in accordance with the objectives of the controller (Ouchi 1980). Therefore, control modes are largely exercised to motivate individuals' behavior. Motivation is well studied as an important factor influencing human behavior (Locke and Latham 2004) and particularly intrinsic motivation has been recognized as a critical antecedent for high quality performance (Utman 1997). This indicates the importance of understanding work-environment characteristics that positively affect individuals' intrinsic motivation. Surprisingly, and to the best of our knowledge, there is limited research and empirical evidence on the relationship between different control modes—as understood in the research stream of Kirsch (1997)—and controlees' motivation.

Motivation generally refers to "*internal factors that impel action and to external factors that can act as inducements to action*" (Locke and Latham 2004, p. 388). According to self-determination theory, motivation is generally classified as extrinsic or intrinsic motivation (Deci and Ryan 1985). Extrinsic motivation refers to a motivation to complete a task or engage in an activity because of its consequences, such as gaining a reward or evading punishment. In contrast, intrinsic motivation is related to individuals' motivation to complete a task or perform an action out of own interest, enjoyment and for the sake of the activity itself (Deci and Ryan 2000). Intrinsic motivation has been found to be superior to other forms of motivation (Carton 1996; Deci and Ryan 2000) and intrinsic motivation plays a predominant role in more open environments (Ke and Zhang 2009). Given that software platforms rely on highly motivated third-party developers who are eager to invest their time and effort into developing and updating apps for the platform, we focus on the role of third-party developers' intrinsic motivation in order to analyze the effects between informal control modes and crucial developer outcomes.

Self-determination theory proposes that it is more likely to perform intrinsically motivated activities when basic psychological needs are satisfied, which make individuals' activities more interesting and more likely to be performed for their own sake. These basic needs refer to individuals' autonomy, competence and relatedness (Deci and Ryan 2000). Autonomy refers to a perceived degree to which an individual performs a task or persuades a goal which is based on own decisions and own desires. Competence is the degree to which an individual can interact effectively with the work environment and the perception of their competence to accomplish desired outcomes. Relatedness is the degree to which individuals feel connected to others and are involved with their social surroundings (Deci and Ryan 2000; Gagne and Deci 2005). On the contrary, situations that undermine individuals' autonomy and make them feel incompetent or rather isolated from their work-environment will weaken their intrinsically motivated behavior. Intrinsic motivation is generally associated with a sense of well-being, higher self-esteem and integrity as well as a higher overall job satisfaction (e.g., Carton 1996; Deci and Ryan 1985; Deci and Ryan 2000; Vallerand and Bissonnette 1992). Indeed, having fun and enjoying an activity is seen as the core of intrinsic motivation (Deci and Ryan 1985).

Previous studies have found that software development is an inherently motivating task, given that it is creative and complicated, but challenging for superiors to observe (Hilkert et al. 2010; Kirsch 1996; Weinberg 1998). In literature on open source software, developers' intrinsic motivation has been examined as a crucial engagement factor for many open source contexts. However, while for example Shah (2006) found evidence that intrinsic motivation is positively related to developers' engagement in a project, Roberts et al. (2006) found no significant effect on developers' contribution level. Nevertheless, open source software contexts are different from our study's context, due to the typically absence of a central platform owner who provides a software core and who steers and controls activities and decisions on and around a software platform. In addition, Amabile et al. (1994) pointed out that individuals' motivation regarding specific activities may vary regarding their surrounding context. Thus, the purpose of our study is to examine third-party developers' intrinsic motivation regarding app development on software platforms. This activity typically includes being exposed to the platform's principal market and governance strategies, interacting with the platform and its community, and employing available development resources.

4.3 Research Model and Hypotheses

In the following, we develop our research model (Figure 4-1). We propose that (1) informal control modes will positively affect third-party developers' intrinsic motivation to develop apps for the platform and (2) their intrinsic motivation mediates the effects of informal control modes on crucial developer outcomes.

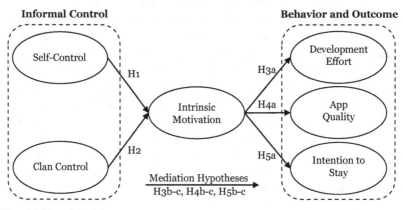

Figure 4-1: Research Model

4.3.1 Informal Control Modes and Intrinsic Motivation

Self-control is based on self-management and self-regulation by the controlee (Kirsch 1997). Controllers implement self-control in their work-environment by giving controlees freedom to decide on their own activities and to choose their own goals in specific areas. Other forms of regulations or monitoring which may result in infringements on individuals' activities are mainly absent and individuals are not urged to comply with pre-specified behaviors or outcomes. Thus, self-control creates a work environment in which individuals have the opportunity to pursuit their self-interests and to satisfy their desire to work autonomously. If individuals perceive a certain amount of autonomy, their activities are likely to be intrinsically motivated and associated with enjoyment and satisfaction (Deci and Ryan 1985). Also, if individuals gain control over their own work, they are likely to perceive their work as meaningful and interesting (Slocum and Sims 1980). Taken to the software platform context, if platform owners grant third-party developers a certain amount of freedom to decide on their own development goals and activities as well as encourage and train developers in exercising self-control, developers are likely to perceive and appreciate a higher degree of autonomy.

This in turn may lead to higher intrinsic motivation during app development on the platform. In summary, these arguments suggest that:

H1: The exercise of self-control is positively related to third-party developers' intrinsic motivation.

Exercising clan control is based on promulgating shared values, norms and beliefs and on reducing different views across individuals, which could be achieved either by the controller or by individuals of the clan (Choudhury and Sabherwal 2003; Kirsch 1997; Rowe and Wright 1997). Exercising clan control builds on regular interactions and information sharing among members of a collective in order to spread these shared values, norms and common goals. Clan control is realized when individuals have internalized common goals and strategies through shared norms and values and therefore have become part of the clan (Kirsch et al. 2002). According to self-determination theory, individuals are more likely to be intrinsically motivated and to enjoy their activities if their basic need for autonomy, competence and/or relatedness is satisfied (Deci and Ryan 2000). Commitment to a group along with a homelike feeling is likely reached by individuals who are working for and with people with similar mindsets and common goals (Das and Teng 2001; Ouchi 1980). Therefore, clan control facilitates a sense of belonging and relatedness with other members of the clan. Members of a clan typically discuss issues and questions openly and share information and knowledge among members (Gopal and Gosain 2010). Thus, clan members have possibilities to share their expertise, express their competence in discussions and shape their working environment. Lastly, individuals exposed to clan control still perceive a fair amount of autonomy and opportunity to pursue their self-interests. The constraint to comply with pre-specified behaviors or outcomes is largely absent. Applied to the platform context, if clan control is successfully exercised and individuals have become part of the platform's community, third-party developers are likely to satisfy their needs for relatedness, competence and autonomy. This in turn is likely to facilitate their intrinsic motivation to develop apps for the platform. Therefore, we suggest:

H2: The exercise of clan control is positively related to third-party developers' intrinsic motivation.

4.3.2 Intrinsic Motivation and Developers' Behaviors and Outcomes

Platform owners commonly strive to leverage competences, skills and innovative capacities of external developers and therefore focus on integrating, motivating and binding developers to the platform (Ceccagnoli et al. 2012). In order to analyze effects on third-party developers' performance outcomes, we adapt a classification from previous literature (Fernandez and Moldogaziev 2012): First, work-related outcomes refer to individuals' effort (i.e., how hard they work) and their willingness to find better ways to work, resulting in higher-quality outcomes (i.e., how smart they work). Second, job-related outcomes refer to a general job satisfaction and loyalty towards their employer. Thus, we are focusing on work-related (i.e., development effort and app quality) and platform-related outcomes (i.e., developers' intention to stay on the platform).

Development Effort

Effort can be defined as the intensity and amount of resources expended on a given task and reflects how hard an individual works (Kanfer 1990). High development effort is likely to enhance third-party developers' outcomes and may manifests itself in how often apps are released and updated.

Individuals with a high intrinsic motivation perform activities for the enjoyment, satisfaction and interest mainly derived from the activity itself, for which they experience also a sense of well-being, higher self-esteem and increased initiatives (Deci and Ryan 1985). Because of such enjoyment and interest in an activity, individuals are willing to devote effort (Deci and Ryan 2000). These positive effects are likely to enhance individuals' expectation that their efforts will lead to positive outcomes (Locke and Latham 2004). Also, their self-interest and autonomy may let them perceive their outcomes depending on their own efforts (Wang and Netemeyer 2002). This is in turn likely to motivate individuals to invest even more time and effort into their activities. Taken to the software platform context, if third-party developers are intrinsically motivated and enjoy developing apps for a platform, they are more likely to try harder and invest more effort into their development activities. Thus, we postulate that:

H3a: Third-party developers' intrinsic motivation is positively related to their app development effort.

We further argue that the relationship between self-control and development effort as well as between clan control and development effort is mediated by third-party developers' intrinsic motivation. As discussed above, encouraging and supporting developers in exercising self-control as well as building a clan and exercising clan control on a software platform may stimulate third-party developers' intrinsic motivation. This higher intrinsic motivation may then empower third-party developers to invest more effort into their activities. We therefore suggest that intrinsic motivation carries the positive effects of self-control and clan control over to developers' effort during app development. Therefore, we postulate:

H3b: Intrinsic motivation mediates the effect of self-control on development effort.

H3c: Intrinsic motivation mediates the effect of clan control on development effort.

App Quality

High quality apps are a particular important performance indicator for software platforms, given that such apps are typically rewarded by the platform's customer base with strong sales and low-quality apps with rather poor sales (Tiwana 2014). On software platforms, such quality is typically reflected by app ratings in the platform store and high ratings are a typical goal for developers and platform owners alike.

Intrinsically motivated behaviors are generally associated with a sense of well-being, higher self-esteem and increased initiatives (e.g., Deci and Ryan 1985) which is likely to lead to a greater attention and focus on a task (Osterloh and Frey 2000). Such intrinsically motivated attention has been found to stimulate individuals to engage in creative processes and to explore new pathways for performing a task, which in turn may lead to better problem solving as well as more creative and higher quality outcomes (Amabile et al. 1990; Reiter-Palmon et al. 1998). Additionally, intrinsically motivated behavior has been found to result in faster learning (Ryan and Deci 2000). In a software platform context, third-party developers who are intrinsically motivated and enjoy developing apps for a platform will have a higher possibility to pay great attention to their development activity and arising problems. This stronger focus and higher creativity is likely to enable newer and better ways to solve problems and produce more reliable and higher-quality apps for the platform. Thus, we hypothesize that:

H4a: Third-party developers' intrinsic motivation is positively related to their app quality.

Accordingly to the above arguments, we believe that when third-party developers perceive higher levels of self-control and clan control, they are more likely to perform app development on a platform out of intrinsic motivation and enjoyment. This in turn may also lead to higher creativity and more attention on their app development processes, which is likely to lead to higher quality apps. Thus, we suggest:

H4b: Intrinsic motivation mediates the effect of self-control on app quality.

H4c: Intrinsic motivation mediates the effect of clan control on quality.

Intention to Stay

A crucial platform-related outcome is third-party developers' intention to stay and constantly participate on a platform in the long run (Boudreau 2012; Ceccagnoli et al. 2012). Developers typically contribute to the platform's productivity, robustness and innovative capacity when they continue to develop and update apps for the platform and engage themselves in the platform's community (Iansiti and Levien 2004a).

As mentioned bevor, individuals who are intrinsically motivated perform a task out of interest, enjoyment and satisfaction (Deci and Ryan 1985). Such motivation is likely to be energized and sustainable over time and is typically reflected in an individual's intention to act (Deci and Ryan 2000). Previous studies have empirically demonstrated the relationship between intrinsic motivation and behavioral intentions regarding system and technology usage. When individuals enjoy using a system, they are likely to accept the system and therefore develop a behavioral intention to further use the system (Davis et al. 1992; Venkatesh and Speier 1999). Adapted to the software platform context, if developers enjoy developing apps for a platform and if they feel more satisfied and comfortable, they are more likely to feel an urge to keep performing this activity. These arguments suggest that third-party developers will have a higher intention to keep contributing to and participating in a software platform, when they feel a higher intrinsic motivation and enjoyment while developing apps for the platform. Thus, we postulate:

H5a: Third-party developers' intrinsic motivation is positively related to their intention to stay on the platform.

Given that third-party developers exposed to self- and clan control are more likely to be intrinsically motivated and to enjoy developing apps for a platform, we again argue that this higher intrinsic motivation will carry the positive effects over to developers' intention to stay on the platform. Therefore:

H5b: Intrinsic motivation mediates the effect of self-control on intention to stay.

H5c: Intrinsic motivation mediates the effect of clan control on intention to stay.

4.4 Research Methodology

4.4.1 Data collection and Sample Description

We created an online survey and collected data with app developers of the Android platform in order to test our hypotheses. Google Inc. introduced the Android platform in 2008. The mobile app platform is a typical two-sided software platform with an operating system, middleware and external and internal applications. With a Software Development Kit, third-party developers are able to develop apps for Android devices and to offer these apps via the Play Store, or the Amazon App-Shop. While Android is mostly free, it is not open source. Google is controlling the Android system, device manufactures and app developers have to rely on or cooperate with Google. The Google Play Store offers several proprietary and non-open software (Bergvall-Kåreborn and Howcroft 2011). In Q4 2014, Android offered 1.43 million apps in the Google Play Store, published by nearly 400,000 app developers, and the Amazon App-Shop about 300,000 apps from nearly 50,000 app developers. 60% more

Android apps were download in Q4 2014 compared to Apple apps and Android holds 76.6% of the mobile market (AppFigures 2015; IDC 2015). Thus, we believe that Android developers are a suitable representation for the mobile app market and for data collection in our study.

With a self-developed web-crawler, and similar to previous app developers studies (Benlian et al. 2015), we collected contact data from random Android developers on the Google Play Store and additional data from their published apps. We sent a link to our survey via mail to about 8,000 app developers. The invitation to the survey and the survey's start page explained the purpose of the study and ensured anonymity and confidentiality of the response data. We also asked to forward the survey invitation to a lead developer in order to obtain survey answers form key informants (Kumar et al. 1993). Developers could win a tablet, an e-book reader or amazon gift-cards as a reward for participation.

Our survey was started by 526 developers, which represents a common response rate in such settings of 6.58%. In total, 236 developers finished our survey, from which we removed 6 cases due to implausible short handling time, resulting in a final sample size of N=230. We tested for a possible non-response bias by comparing Chi-squares of the responses from the first quartile and those of the last quartile and found no significant difference between these groups on our main constructs (Armstrong and Overton 1977). This suggests that non-response bias is unlikely to be an issue in our study. Most participants are hobbyist and private app developers (40.9%) or self-employed (33%).

Table 4-1: Sample Demographic (N=230)

Gender	N	%	Experience in software dev.	N	%
Male	214	95.1%	< 1 year	21	9.1%
Female	11	4.8%	1 to 3 years	39	17.0%
Age	**N**	**%**	3 to 5 years	30	13.0%
15-24	41	17.8%	5 to 7 years	26	11.3%
25-34	89	38.7%	> 7 years	114	49.6%
35-44	62	27%	**Experience in app dev.**	**N**	**%**
44-64	37	16.1%	< 1 year	24	9.1%
65+	1	0.4%	1 to 3 years	100	43. 5%
Employment	**N**	**%**	3 to 5 years	66	28.7%
Employed (company)	43	18.7%	5 to 7 years	24	10.4%
Independent/freelancer	17	7.4%	> 7 years	19	8.3%)
Hobbyist or private	94	40.9%	**Number of dev. apps for ...**	**Mean**	**SD**
Self-employed	67	33.0%	... Android	7,29	9.83
Multiple Platforms	**N**	**%**	... Apple	2.47	6.13
Yes	113	49.1%	... Windows Phone	0.65	3.55
No	117	50.9%	... Blackberry	0.21	1.67

The majority has more than 5 years of experience in software development and between 1 and 5 years in app development. Developers in our sample have developed mostly for Android with an average of 7.29 developed apps, while 49.1% have developed as least one app for another platform. Sample demographics are shown in Table 4-1.

4.4.2 Measurement of Constructs

All measures in our survey (see Table 4-2) were based on established scales from previous studies and were slightly revised to make them more fitting and understandable for the study context. Measures for self-control and clan control were adapted from Tiwana and Keil (2009), which are based on the original control measures of prior studies from Kirsch et al. (2002). We added one more item for self-control in order to capture if developers' self-regulation is not caused by an act of ignoring platform rules. We similarly added one more item for clan control in order to capture if shared norms, values and common goals influence developers' procedures and outcomes.

Table 4-2: Measurement Items

Self-Control (Kirsch et al. 2002; Tiwana and Keil 2009)	I self-manage my app development process on the platform.
	I set specific goals for my app project without the platform owner's involvement.
	I define specific procedures for my app project's activities without the platform owner's involvement.
	The platform owner grants autonomy to set goals independently.
Clan Control (Kirsch et al. 2002; Tiwana and Keil 2009)	I attempt to interact regularly with other developers on the Android platform (e.g., in forums, chats, blogs).
	I attempt to understand the platform's goals, values and norms.
	I place a significant weight on understanding the platform's goals, values, and norms.
	I actively participate in developer forums, channels or conferences to understand the platform's goals, values and norms.
	Shared norms, values and goals of the platform influence my app development (procedures, outcomes, etc.).
Intrinsic Motivation (Deci and Ryan 2002)	I enjoy developing apps for the Android platform.
	I would describe developing apps for the Android platform as very interesting.
	Developing apps for the Android platform is fun to do.
Development Effort (Deci and Ryan 2002)	I put a lot of effort into developing apps for the Android platform.
	It is important to me to do well at developing apps for the Android platform.
	I try very hard on developing good apps for the Android platform.
Intention to Stay (Agarwal and Karahanna 2000)	I plan to use the Android platform for app development in the future.
	I intend to continue using the Android platform for app development in the future.
	I expect my use of the Android platform for app development in the future.

Note: All items measured with a 7-point Likert scale, anchored at (1) strongly disagree and (7) strongly agree.

Measures for intrinsic motivation and development effort were adapted from the Intrinsic Motivation Inventory (www.selfdeterminatoitheory.org), initially developed by Deci and Ryan, and which has been used and shown to be stable in several previous studies (e.g., Deci et al. 1994; Ryan 1982). Previous studies have found, that some items within these subscales overlap considerably and therefore may be reduced to less items (Ryan 1982; Wilde et al. 2009). For intrinsic motivation, we adapted three items from the interest/enjoyment subscale, which is seen as the self-reported measure of intrinsic motivation (Deci and Ryan 2002), and for development effort, we adapted three items from the effort subscale. Both measures were revised to capture app development on a specific platform (i.e., activity and context). Measures for intention to stay were based on the behavioral intention construct of Agarwal and Karahanna (2000) and were adjusted to the general platform context. For app quality, we draw on objective data from our web crawler, averaging the rating scores of developers' app portfolio in the Google Play Store. In addition, we included control variables to account for alternative explanations. We included participants' age and gender, years of experience in app-development and size of their app portfolio in the platform store, i.e. the number of published apps.

4.5 Data Analysis and Results

We used structural equation model (SEM) with partial least squares (PLS) to test our research hypotheses. PLS allows for simultaneous testing of the measurement model (i.e., the psychometric properties of the measurement scales) and the estimation of the structural model (i.e., the strength and direction of the relationship between the variables) (Chin 1998). PLS has an added advantage over covariance-based methods (e.g., LISREL) in that it (1) maximizes the explained variance of endogenous variables in the structural model, which enables to understand the amount of variance explained in the constructs and (2) PLS does not make distributional assumptions for the data (Chin 1998). We used the software SmartPLS 2.0. M3 (Ringle et al. 2005). For robust PLS calculation, a minimum sample size of ten times the maximum number of any paths in the model is suggested (Hair et al. 2012), which our data exceeded with N=230. For assessing the significance levels of the paths, we used a bootstrapping procedure with no sign changes and 1,000 resamples following recommendations by Hair et al. (2012). In a two-step approach, we first assessed our measurement model and then analyzed our hypotheses.

4.5.1 Assessment of Measurement Model

We assessed content validity, convergent validity and discriminant validity for all our latent reflective constructs, according to guidelines by Gefen and Straub (2005). For content validity, we performed a qualitative pre-test with developers in order to detect ambiguities, which resulted in some minor wording changes. For convergent validity we used three criteria recommended by Fornell and Larcker (1981): First, all measurement factor loadings must be significant and above the threshold value of 0.70; second, composite reliabilities should exceed 0.80; and third, the average variance extracted (AVE) by each construct must exceed the variance due to measurement error for that construct (i.e., AVE should exceed 0.50). All factor loadings of the measurement items were significant (all $p < .001$) and above the recommended threshold value, with one exception. One item of clan control loaded slightly below the recommended threshold (0.671), which is, however, still in an acceptable range (Chin 1998). Furthermore, every item loaded highest on its construct and cross-loadings differences were much higher than the recommended threshold value of 0.1 (Gefen and Straub 2005). The constructs composite reliabilities were all above 0.885 and the values for AVE were all higher than 0.692. Thus, all constructs met the norms of convergent validity (see Table 4-3).

Table 4-3: Reliability, validity, and distribution statistics of latent variable scores

Constructs	Mean (SD)	Loading Range	Composite Reliability	Average Variance Extracted
Self-Control	6.17 (1.06)	0.777 - 0.891	0.901	0.692
Clan Control	4.73 (1.46)	0.671 - 0.901	0.922	0.711
Intrinsic Motivation	5.62 (1.15)	0.919 - 0.937	0.944	0.858
Development Effort	5.73 (1.09)	0.796 - 0.870	0.885	0.715
Intention to Stay	6.25 (1.11)	0.925 - 0.981	0.970	0.916
App Quality	4.01 (0.94)	Single-item		

Table 4-4: Square root of AVE (bolded cells) and correlations of latent variable scores

	Constructs	1	2	3	4	5	6
1	Self-Control	**0.83**					
2	Clan Control	0.04	**0.84**				
3	Intrinsic Motivation	0.19	0.40	**0.93**			
4	Development Effort	0.26	0.39	0.42	**0.85**		
5	Intention to Stay	0.27	0.23	0.37	0.22	**0.96**	
6	App Quality	0.11	0.09	0.19	0.09	-0.06	-

For discriminant validity, the square root correlation between a pair of constructs should be less than the AVE of each construct (Fornell and Larcker 1981). All correlations among constructs are less than the square root of AVE (see Table 4-4), indicating evidence for discriminant validity. Given that our data was collected in the same time period, we also checked for possible common method bias (Podsakoff et al. 2003). Harman's one factor test revealed that a single factor could not explain most of the variance among the model variables; the first factor explained only 29.07%. We also compared construct correlations (Pavlou et al. 2007), revealing that no constructs related over 0.9. Both indicate that common method bias is unlikely to exist. All results suggest that the constructs are theoretical and empirical distinguishable concepts with good measurement properties.

4.5.2 Hypotheses Testing

We first tested for alternative explanations by analyzing the effects of our control variables on the model's dependent variables. We did not find any significant effects of age, gender, experience in app development or portfolio size on development effort, app quality or intention to stay (all p >.05), with one exception. Experience in app development had a positive and significant impact on development effort (β = .15; p < .05) which, however, explained only a low amount of variance. The results of the structural model analysis are shown in Figure 2.

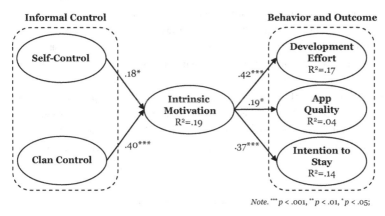

Figure 4-2: Results of PLS SEM Analysis

The model explained 19% of the variance in intrinsic motivation, 17% of the variance in development effort, 14% of the variance in intention to stay and only 4% of variance in app quality. Regarding the effects of informal control modes on intrinsic motivation, we found that self-control had a positive significant effect on intrinsic motivation (β = .18; p < .05), which supported H1. Furthermore, clan control had a strong positive significant effect on intrinsic motivation (β = .40; p < .001), in support of H2. Regarding the effects of intrinsic motivation on developers' behaviors and outcomes, we found that intrinsic motivation had a positive and significant effect on development effort (β = .42; p < .001), supporting H3a. We also found a positive significant effect of intrinsic motivation on app quality (β = .19; p < .05), which supported H4a. Finally, and as expected, we found that intrinsic motivation had a positive significant effect on developers' intention to stay (β = .37; p < .001), supporting H5a.

Given that clan control exhibited a remarkably stronger effect on intrinsic motivation than self-control, we further investigated the differential effects of both informal control modes on third-party developers' intrinsic motivation. Following procedures by Sarstedt and Wilczynski (2009), we compared bootstrapping results for the path coefficients based on paired t-tests. The results showed that the effect of clan-control on third-party developers intrinsic motivation ($\beta = .40$; $p < .001$) is consistently and significantly stronger (t-value = 77.67; $p <$ .001) than the effect of self-control on intrinsic motivation ($\beta = .18$; $p < .05$).

4.5.3 Mediation Analysis

In order to test for a mediating effect of third-party developers' intrinsic motivation, we performed a two-step approach, following recommendations by Preacher and Hayes (2008). In step 1, we analyzed the direct effects of self-control and clan control on development effort, app quality and intention to stay without the mediator intrinsic motivation. In step 2, we introduced intrinsic motivation into the model and analyzed the full path model. In step 1, the model explained 22% of the variance in development effort, 12% of the variance in intention to stay and only 2% of the variance in app quality. We found a positive significant effect of self-control on development effort ($\beta = .25$; $p < .001$) and of self-control on intention to stay ($\beta = .26$; $p < .01$). However, the effect of self-control on app quality was not significant ($\beta = .11$; $p > .05$). Regarding clan control, we found a positive significant effect of clan control on development effort ($\beta = .39$; $p < .001$) and of clan control on intention to stay ($\beta = .22$; $p < .01$). Then again, we could not find a significant effect of clan control on app quality ($\beta = .08$; $p > .05$).

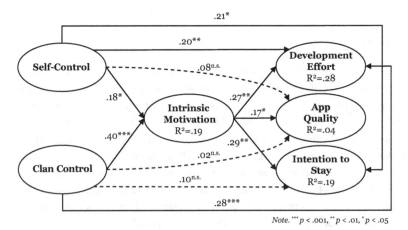

Note. $^{***}p < .001$, $^{**}p < .01$, $^{*}p < .05$

Figure 4-3: Final Model of the Mediation Analysis

In step 2 (see Figure 4-3), we introduced our mediator intrinsic motivation into the model. Due to the significant effects of intrinsic motivation, the explained variance increased in development effort (R^2=.28), intention to stay (R^2= .19) and app quality (R^2=.04) compared to the analysis in step 1. First, we found a positive significant effect of intrinsic motivation on development effort (β = .27; p < .01). The effect of self-control on development effort decreased but remained significant (β = .20; p < .01) and also the effect of clan control on development effort decreased but remained significant (β = .28; p < .001). Therefore, intrinsic motivation partially mediated the effect of both self-control and clan control on development effort in support of H3b and H3c. Second, we also found a significant positive effect of intrinsic motivation on intention to stay (β = .29; p < .01). The effect of self-control on intention to stay decreased slightly but remained significant (β = .21; p < .05), while the effect of clan control on intention to stay decreased and became non-significant (β = .10; p > .05). This suggests that intrinsic motivation partially mediated the effect of self-control on intention to stay and fully mediated the effect of clan control. This supports H5b and H5c. Finally, because there were no significant effects of self-control and clan control on app quality, intrinsic motivation did not mediate the effects form self-control and clan control on app quality. Therefore, H4b and H4c had to be rejected. Table 4-5 summarizes the results of our hypotheses testing.

Table 4-5: Summary of Hypotheses Testing

H1	Self-Control → Intrinsic Motivation	supported
H2	Clan Control → Intrinsic Motivation	supported
H3a	Intrinsic Motivation -> Development Effort	supported
H3b	Self-Control → Intrinsic Motivation → Development Effort	supported
H3c	Clan Control → Intrinsic Motivation → Development Effort	supported
H4a	Intrinsic Motivation → App Quality	supported
H4b	Self-Control → Intrinsic Motivation → App Quality	not supported
H4c	Clan Control → Intrinsic Motivation → App Quality	not supported
H5a	Intrinsic Motivation → Intention to Stay	supported
H5b	Self-Control → Intrinsic Motivation → Intention to Stay	supported
H5c	Clan Control → Intrinsic Motivation → Intention to Stay	supported

Similar to above, we additionally examined the differential effects of self- and clan control on third-party developers effort and intention to stay, following again procedures by Sarstedt and Wilczynski (2009). The results showed that the effect of clan control on development effort is consistently and significantly stronger than the effect of self-control (t-value = 26.51; p < .001). Furthermore, the effect of self-control is consistently and significantly stronger on developers' intention to stay compared to the effect of clan control (t-value = 31.95; p < .001).

Given the rather low variances explained in our dependent variables, we further analyzed different effect sizes (f^2, q^2) and the predictive relevance (based on Stone-Geisser-Q^2) in our final model, following guidelines by Cohen (1988). The f^2 effect size reports the change in the R^2 when a specific exogenous construct is omitted from the model. Table 4-6 shows that f^2 effect sizes in our model are mostly small (> 0.02) or medium (> 0.15), with minor exceptions where we have to assume negligible influence (< 0.02). Further, we analyzed the predictive relevance (Q^2) of our model with respect to the endogenous variables. Table 4-6 shows, all Q^2 values are above zero, thus providing support for the predictive relevance for the model's endogenous constructs. The q^2 effect sizes for the predictive relevance are mostly small (> 0.02) or medium (> 0.15), with minor exceptions where we have to assume no predictive relevance (< 0.02).

Table 4-6: Variance Explained (R^2), Predictive Relevance (Q^2) and Effect Size (f^2 and q^2)

	Intrinsic Motivation		Developer Effort		App Quality		Intention to Stay	
	R^2	Q^2	R^2	Q^2	R^2	Q^2	R^2	Q^2
	.194	.163	.275	.193	.041	.050	.190	.171
	f^2	q^2	f^2	q^2	f^2	q^2	f^2	q^2
Self-Control	.038	.024	.052	.029	.006	0.036	0.053	0.047
Clan Control	.194	.156	.091	.052	.000	0.005	0.010	0.021
Intrinsic Motivation	-	-	.072	.047	.023	0.044	0.084	0.072

4.6 Discussion and Conclusion

The objective of this paper was to better understand the effects of self-control and clan control in a software platform context. We focused on the mediating role of third-party developers' intrinsic motivation in the relationship between informal control modes and developers' effort, app quality and intention to stay on a platform. First, our study results demonstrate that both self-control and clan control positively influence third-party developers' intrinsic motivation to develop apps on the platform. Conversely, developers are likely to have a lower intrinsic motivation if they perceive decisions and activities on a platform less originated by themselves and refuse to regularly interact and share common norms, values and goals with the platform and its community. In addition, our findings indicate that clan control is more conducive in shaping third-party developers' intrinsic motivation compared to self-control. Second, our study revealed that third-party developers' intrinsic motivation enhances crucial developer outcomes, behaviors and intentions on software platforms. Particular, developers with a higher intrinsic motivation to develop apps for the platform invest more time and effort in their app development procedures, are more likely to have higher quality apps in the platform store and are more willing to stay on the platform and keep developing apps for the platform. Finally, and most important, our mediation analysis revealed an explanatory mechanism for why self-control and clan control operate beneficially on software platforms. Third-party developers' intrinsic motivation serves as a mediator, carrying the positive effects of self-control and clan control over to developers' effort and intention to stay on the platform. In other words, third-party developers exposed to self-control and clan control are likely to foster a higher intrinsic motivation to develop apps for the platform, which ultimately leads to higher development effort and a higher intention to stay on the platform. However, the explained variances and effect sizes in our structural model are rather small, revealing a tension between our theoretical development and the study's results. Other factors we did not account for may have overridden the effects of intrinsic motivation. For example, third-party developers' extrinsic motivation (i.e., selling apps and earning money) may have stronger effects on third-party developers' behaviors and outcomes. In order to gain a deeper understanding of control modes in software platform contexts and for maximizing the model's explanatory power, future studies are advised to reproduce our findings and include additional constructs (i.e., in particular app developers' extrinsic motivation).

In addition to the study's key findings, other results of our mediation analysis are worth discussing. Given that we could not find a direct effect from self-control and clan control on app quality in the mediation analysis, we could not identify a mediating effect of intrinsic motivation in this relation. However, due to positive significant effects from intrinsic motivation on app quality, intrinsic motivation still plays a role between informal control modes and developers' app quality. Furthermore, the direct effects from self-control and clan control on development effort and self-control on intention to stay remained significant, thus intrinsic motivation only partially mediated these effects. On the one hand, this again demonstrates the importance and positive effects of self-control and clan control on software platforms, even without the underlying explanatory mechanism of third-party developers' intrinsic motivation. On the other hand, these results call for further research in order to detect other mediators and explanatory arguments besides intrinsic motivation regarding the relationship between informal control modes and crucial developer behaviors and outcomes.

4.6.1 Theoretical and Practical Implications

Our study suggests a number of interesting implications. From a theoretical point of view, the study findings provide a deeper understanding of the effects of informal control modes on software platforms. First, our study addresses an important gap in IS control literature by analyzing the relationship between control modes and an individual's motivation, which, to the best of our knowledge, has not yet been empirically tested and established in IS research. More specifically, our study demonstrates that both self-control and clan control on software platforms are positively related to third-party developers' intrinsic motivation. Moreover, we could show that clan control is more conducive for third-party developers' intrinsic motivation compared to self-control. Assumed that an overemphasis of self-control could also lead to coordination and performance problems (Slocum and Sims 1980), our study suggests that clan control is the superior choice of informal control on software platforms. This is because clan control grants a certain amount of autonomy while simultaneously bringing developers onto a common path of shared values, beliefs and goals, without the need for tight supervision and regulation.

Second, our study provides evidence that third-party developers' intrinsic motivation serves as a mediator, carrying the positive effects of self-control and clan control over to developers' effort and their intention to stay on the platform. Thus, our study addresses another important gap, given that only a few studies have investigated important downstream effects of control modes, which, in addition, have largely focused on formal control without providing insights into underlying explanatory processes. By identifying third-party developers' intrinsic motivation as an underlying explanatory argument of why informal control modes positively affect developers' behaviors and outcomes, our study contributes to advancing control literature (Kirsch 1997; Ouchi 1979). Moreover, our study demonstrates that even without exercising conventional formal control modes, high performance outcomes are possible. Therefore, our study not only contributes to the ongoing discussion about "more control is better" (Tiwana 2010), but also responds to calls for research on analyzing governance mechanisms in dynamic and fast-growing platform ecosystems, especially with a focus on hitherto underexplored informal control modes (Tiwana et al. 2013; Wareham et al. 2014). Third, we also contribute to motivation literature. While motivation literature and self-determination theory has a long tradition in organizational contexts, only a few studies have analyzed motivational factors in software platform contexts. Given the limited studies in this area and mixed results regarding developers' intrinsic motivation in open source software development contexts (e.g., Roberts et al. 2006; Shah 2006), our study further advances the body of knowledge regarding antecedents of platform developers' intrinsic motivation and how this motivation affects their behaviors and outcomes. Finally, our study reveals a tension between the theoretical development and the rather moderate strength of the study results. We therefore provide new research opportunities for future studies to investigate alternative explanations for developers' performance outcomes, i.e. developers' extrinsic motivation, in order to maximize the model's explanatory power.

Beyond these theoretical implications, our study provides practical implications for platform owners as well. First, our study results demonstrate that self-control and especially clan control is positively related to third-party developers' intrinsic motivation, which leads to higher development effort and a higher intention to stay on the platform. Therefore, in order to utilize competences and skills of external and to integrate, motivate and keep developers on the platform, platform owners are advised to increasingly exercise and choose areas for self-control and clan control. Our study shows that even without exercising conventional tight formal control modes, high performance outcomes are possible. Platform owners are therefore advised to exercise more soft-power instruments, i.e. self- and clan control, instead of hard-power instruments (Yoffie and Kwak 2006). Platform owners may encourage and support third-party developers in exercising self-control by structuring the platform environment appropriately, providing crucial informational cues and statistics necessary for making self-directed decisions, offering trainings for self-management and examples for possible best-practice behaviors and decisions. For clan control, platform owners are advised to promulgate shared norms, values and common goals which are beneficial for the platform and to set an example of best practice and desired work-related behaviors and outcomes. They may participate in developer communities and spread desired platform goals, beliefs and market strategies with newsletters, publications for developers or dedicated conferences. Moreover, in order to build a strong platform community (or clan), platform owners could provide an ecosystem which simplifies collaboration and communication between third-party developers in order to spread such shared norms, values and goals. Developer forums, chats and conferences as well as solution-oriented wikis and blogs may help developers to interact with each other and to build social relations in the community. Moreover, third-party developers are advised to choose platforms with a more open and self-regulating governance structure in order to maximize their freedom and intrinsic motivation. App developers may try to understand the norms, values and common goals of a platform an incorporate these into their development activities. Interacting with the platform's community and following shared values and common goals may help them to become part of a platform clan, positively affect their intrinsic motivation and lead to higher development effort and a higher intention to stay on the platform.

4.6.2 Limitations and Future Work

While our study offers several important contributions, it is important to evaluate the results and implications in the light of its limitations. First, our study was focused on app developers of the Android platform and our survey was completed by mostly hobbyist, private or self-employed developers. While we believe that Android developers are a good representative of the mobile app industry, external validity of the study results is limited and may be not applicable to other platforms or employed app developers. Future studies are advised to analyze informal control modes and developers' intrinsic motivation across different platforms, such as Apple's App Store or Facebook's App Center, including a broader mix of employed and private third-party developers. Given that control mechanisms vary across different platform types, future studies may also include open source platform contexts. A result comparison of different platforms could also provide relevant insights for platform governance literature. Second, and as mentioned above, we are aware that the study's structural model explained only a low amount of variance. As an explanation, other factors we did not account for may have overridden some effects, and regarding app quality, the used measurement may not reflect the true quality of developers' apps. While our study is, to the best of our knowledge, the first to establish the link between control modes and intrinsic motivation, future studies may extend the study's model by including and comparing different types of control and motivation. Future studies may analyze and compare the differential effects of formal and informal control modes as well as their interaction effects in a portfolio of control modes (Kirsch 1997). Regarding third-party developers' motivation, future studies are advised to analyze intrinsic motivation in more detail by separately measuring developers' perceived autonomy, competence and relatedness as well as different forms of extrinsic motivation into their analysis. Future studies may also include additional endogenous variables and alternative measurements in order to improve the models' explanatory power.

4.6.3 Conclusion

Software platforms rely heavily on highly motivated third-party developers who are eager to invest their time and effort into developing and updating apps for the platform. The myriad of third-party developers, apps and development projects on software platforms have increased the importance of exercising informal control as part of platform governance. However, our knowledge regarding the effects of such control modes in platform settings is still limited and underlying explanations are largely missing. By integrating control and motivational theory, our study provides a deeper understanding of the positive effects of self-control and clan control in software platform settings and reveals a mediating role of third-party developers' intrinsic motivation on developers' effort and intention to stay on a platform. Clan control was found to be particularly beneficial in shaping developers' intrinsic motivation and developer performance on software platforms. Despite our comprehensive findings, we believe that our study took only initial steps and that analyzing the effects of informal control on software platforms and third-party developers' motivations as an underlying explanatory mechanism is still a rich avenue for future research. We hope that our study was able to provide new insights and ideas in order to further advance IS research on software platform governance and control.

Chapter 5: Social Capital and Clan Control on Software Platforms

Title: How Social Capital Facilitates Clan Control on Software Platforms to Enhance
App-Developers' Performance and Success

Authors: Goldbach, Tobias, Technische Universität Darmstadt, Germany
Benlian, Alexander, Technische Universität Darmstadt, Germany

Published in: International Conference on Information Systems (ICIS 2015),
December 13-16, 2015, Fort Worth, United States

Abstract

Although platform operators such as Google or Apple are facing a trade-off between retaining
and relinquishing control to manage a myriad of third-party developers and development
projects, little is known about how clan control—a particularly relevant informal control
mode in decentralized multi-project software development—can be facilitated on software
platforms and how it affects developer performance. Drawing on control literature and social
capital theory, we conducted an online survey with 218 app developers of Google's Android
platform in which we examined how social capital facilitates the exercise of clan control to
enhance crucial developer performance outcomes. Our study not only shows that all three
dimensions of social capital (i.e., structural, cognitive and relational social capital) are critical
levers for exercising clan control on software platforms, but also that clan control leads to
higher development performance and app ratings on the platform. Theoretical and practical
implications are discussed.

Keywords: Clan Control, Social Capital, Developer Performance, Software Platforms

5.1 Introduction

Over the past few years, software platforms and their corresponding ecosystems (Jansen et al. 2009) have radically changed the software industry. Platform owners deliberately open their ecosystems and enable external developers to add functionality to the core product of the platform (Boudreau 2012) and therefore utilize competences and innovative capacities of an external developer community (Ceccagnoli et al. 2012) in order to respond to rapidly changing markets and customer needs (Boudreau and Lakhani 2009). A software platform is defined as *"the extensible codebase of a software-based system that provides core functionality shared by the modules that interoperate with it and the interfaces through which they interoperate"* (Tiwana et al. 2010). Mobile platforms (e.g., Apple's App Store or Google's Play Store) have seen a massive growth in offered applications (apps), third-party developers, overall revenues and market size. Google nearly doubled the number of offered apps in their Play Store to 1.43 million apps from Q4/2013 to Q4/2014, published by nearly 400,000 developers. Apple developers have earned a cumulative $25 billion from their app sales since the App Store was introduced in 2008 (Apple 2015). Shipments of smartphones worldwide have grown by a stunning 27.7% in 2014 to 1.3 billion (IDC 2015).

From the view of platform governance, platform owners are challenged to align the numerous and diverse goals and behaviors of third-party developers with the platform's strategies (Tiwana et al. 2010). Control theory (Kirsch 1997; Ouchi 1980) has often been invoked in order to describe and analyze the alignment between two parties. Control is defined as a set of mechanisms a controller uses to influence controlees to act in accordance with the controller's objectives (Ouchi 1980). Clan control, a key informal control mode which is based on interactions and influences among clan members, has been found to be essential in complex IT projects (Kirsch 2004; Kohli and Kettinger 2004). In particular, clan control is fundamentally important for more open and dynamic contexts (Kirsch et al. 2010), such as in software platforms. This is because decentralized and multi-project software development makes it difficult, costly and time-consuming to specify and measure each individual's behaviors and outcomes (Kirsch 2004; Tiwana et al. 2010). With clan control, behaviors are motivated and influenced by shared values, norms and common goals, which have to be promulgated, understood and further shared by individuals of the clan (Ouchi 1979). Clan control therefore relies on social interactions, relationships and information sharing. These are as well essential elements of social capital, which is defined as the actual and potential resources embedded within and derived from social relations (Nahapiet and Ghoshal 1998). Third-party developers typically participate in platform-dedicated online communities to interact with each other and to organize themselves in a clan. A clan can be seen as a group with strong social capital (Chua et al. 2012) and social capital has been found to be a suitable concept for analyzing the nature of clan control (Kirsch et al. 2010).

In IS control research, two research gaps are particular noteworthy. First, studies have largely focused on understanding the nature, antecedents and choice of formal and informal control modes (e.g., Choudhury and Sabherwal 2003; Henderson and Lee 1992; Kirsch 1996; Kirsch 1997; Kirsch et al. 2002) and only a few studies analyzed the resulting effects of control modes (Goldbach et al. 2014; Gopal and Gosain 2010; Keil et al. 2013; Tiwana 2010; Tiwana and Keil 2009). Despite the agreement of previous studies about the importance of clan control for complex IT projects (Kirsch 2004; Kohli and Kettinger 2004), these studies focused mostly on formal control modes or resulted in mixed findings regarding the effects of clan control (Gopal and Gosain 2010; Tiwana 2010). Studies that explicitly zoomed in on clan control identified social capital as an important antecedent of clan control, but neglected to ascertain whether facilitated clan control indeed increased downstream performance outcomes (Chua et al. 2012; Kirsch et al. 2010). As a second research gap, most of IS control studies have either focused on internal projects (Cardinal 2001; Chua et al. 2012; Kirsch 1996; Kirsch 2004; Kirsch et al. 2010) or outsourced projects (Gregory et al. 2013; Rustagi et al. 2008; Srivastava and Teo 2012; Tiwana and Keil 2009). Studies in more open settings have analyzed the relationship between control and boundary resources on the Apple platform (Ghazawneh and Henfridsson 2013), or the relation between control and autonomy in a business technology ecosystem (Wareham et al. 2014). However, our knowledge regarding how social capital facilitates clan control and how such facilitated clan control translates into performance outcomes is still limited. We build our study on previous research (Chua et al. 2012; Kirsch et al. 2010), analyzing social capital as a facilitator of clan control in a more open and dynamic software platform context and investigating the resulting effects on crucial developer outcomes. The study's purpose is therefore to analyze how third-party developers' social capital on software platforms facilitates the exercise of clan control in order to enhance developers' performance and app success, guided by our research questions:

(1) *How does social capital facilitate the exercise of clan control on software platforms?*

(2) *How does clan control enhance app developers' performance outcomes on software platforms?*

We conducted an online survey with 218 mobile app developers of Google's Android platform. Our study shows that each dimension of social capital (i.e., structural, cognitive and relational social capital) facilitates the exercise of clan control and that clan control, in turn, enhances developer- and app-related performance outcomes. By analyzing the facilitators and effects of clan control in a software platform context, our study contributes to IS control theory, which has contributed a rich literature in organizational contexts but is still relatively unexplored on software platforms (e.g., Manikas and Jansen 2013; Tiwana et al. 2010). Our study particularly advances platform governance literature by responding to several calls for research (Tiwana et al. 2013; Wareham et al. 2014) on how to shape control in platform settings and on how clan control influences developer behaviors and outcomes. Further, our study demonstrates that positive effects of social capital on clan control are carried over to enhance developers' performance outcomes and that even in—or perhaps, especially in—decentralized multi-project software development contexts social capital plays a central role in facilitating clan control.

The remainder of the paper is structured as follows. First, the theoretical background of our paper is laid out, followed by our research model and hypotheses. Next, we describe our research methodology and results of our online survey. In the concluding section, we discuss the implications of the results for research and practice and point out the paper's limitations as well as promising areas for future research.

5.2 Theoretical Background

5.2.1 Platform Control and the Conceptualization of Clan Control

Harmonizing the platform owners' own strategies and objectives with third-party developers' goals and activities is one of the main challenges of platform governance. Tiwana et al. (2010) define platform governance from a decision-making perspective as who makes what decision on and about a platform. This includes the ownership of the platform and its modules, the allocation of decision rights between a platform owner and external developers, and finally, how behaviors and outcomes are controlled on a platform. Control theory and the right choice of control modes are thus an important part of platform governance. However, software platforms are distinct from traditional developer environments in corporations and other more structured work settings. Platform owners and third-party developers are typically in a less hierarchical and less compulsory relationship. As a reason, the vast number of external developers makes it prohibitively costly and time-consuming to exercise tight control on each development project (Tiwana et al. 2010). Further, the interests and goals of participants in platform ecosystems are not necessarily incongruent, given that both parties are interested in increasing the platform's installed customer base and in generating revenues (Tiwana 2014). More importantly, third-party developers predominantly make their own decisions in terms of their strategies, project requirements and development activities (Bergvall-Kåreborn and Howcroft 2011). Thus, self-directed work is given more weight in platform environments than in traditional software development contexts. However, a wide variety of control modes are actually observed on software platforms (e.g., Tiwana 2014).

Control is defined as controller's attempts to influence and motivate an individual or a group (the controlee) to act in accordance with the objectives of the controller (Ouchi 1980). Control mechanisms are typically divided into formal control and informal control modes (e.g., Kirsch

1997; Kirsch et al. 2002): On the one hand, formal control refers to behavior control (or process control) and outcome control. With formal control, desirable behaviors or outcomes are determined by controllers in advance, for instance, by written contracts. Adherence to these pre-specifications is monitored, evaluated and sanctioned or rewarded by the controller accordingly (Kirsch et al. 2002). Mobile platform providers for example pre-specify the look and feel of an app, programming tools for the development process or approve apps for selling in the platform's market store. Informal control modes, on the other hand, refer to social or people skills and self-regulation, building on shared norms and values of individuals and groups. Informal control modes are divided into self-control and clan control. With self-control, individuals set their own goals, monitor themselves and sanction or reward themselves in accordance. In this respect, controllers (e.g., platform providers) may build a self-regulatory environment by providing needed tools and trainings that allow controlees to organize themselves, make their own decisions and evaluate themselves based on their own performance (Kirsch et al. 2002). In this study, our research interest lies on clan control, given its crucial role as soft power instrument for platform providers to bring autonomous developers onto a common path, which is of particular importance in decentralized and complex multi-project contexts (Kirsch 2004; Tiwana et al. 2010; Yoffie and Kwak 2006).

A clan is a homogeneous group where members are dependent on each other and share common values, beliefs, and norms, which influence their behaviors and outcomes (Ouchi and Price 1978). According to Chua et al. (2012), clan control is either implemented to leverage an existing clan or to build and develop a new clan. Shared values, norms and common goals are not only propagated by a controller but also emerge and are encouraged by members of an effective clan (Kirsch 1997; Turner and Makhija 2006). Clan control has been found to be especially relevant when outcomes are unclear or difficult to measure and behavior is hard to specify or not observable (Kirsch 1996; Kirsch et al. 2002; Kohli and Kettinger 2004). However, although software platforms are characterized by a highly dynamic and unstructured environment with a myriad of developers and numerous development projects (Tiwana et al. 2010), little is known about how clan control can be facilitated on software platforms and how clan control effects developers' performance outcomes. Previous research on the downstream effects of control have primarily focused on formal control modes and the few studies that looked at the consequences of clan control produced only limited or inconclusive findings (Gopal and Gosain 2010; Keil et al. 2013; Tiwana 2010; Tiwana and Keil 2009).

As a typical venue for creating clan control on software platforms, platform-dedicated online communities (e.g., developer.apple.com or developer.android.com) usually serve third-party developers to interact with each other, to share information and to organize themselves. Other opportunities for sharing information, knowledge, expertise and best practices include forums, wikis, blogs, chats and the participation at developer conferences (Bergvall-Kåreborn and Howcroft 2011). However, developers are not per se part of a clan on a platform. Developers may develop apps entirely on their own without interacting or sharing common norms and goals with the platform community. Clan control is exercised on a software platform, when app developers attempt to understand and place a significant weight on understanding common platform values, norms and as well as participate in the developer community to become a regular member of the clan (Kirsch et al. 2002). Platform owners may promulgate norms, values and goals that are beneficial for the platform. These may be platform strategies and characteristics that attract customers and developers, app features that contribute to the needs of the customer base or behaviors regarding app updates and bug fixing. As an example for clan control on software platforms, Apple products are promoted as being innovative, well designed and trendy, which is reflected in their usability, design, and user experience. Apple's customers and app developers mainly share these norms and values, which in turn is manifested in high-quality designs of third-party apps. Android, on the other side, is a more open and free platform, aiming at a wide variety of devices, diversity in offered apps and customizability for customers, which emerges in developers' behaviors and outcomes for the platform. (Bergvall-Kåreborn and Howcroft 2011; Tiwana 2014). Common norms and goals in a development context may also be the adherence to coding and design standards, naming conventions, testing processes and framework usage.

5.2.2 Social Capital on Software Platforms

In order to understand, spread and adapt shared norms, values and common goals in a collective, clan control depends on social interactions, relationships and information sharing among clan members (Ouchi 1979). For analyzing social relationships in IS research, the concept of Nahapiet and Ghoshal (1998) is the most widely accepted and has been widely used in previous studies (e.g., Chua et al. 2012; Kirsch et al. 2010). Nahapiet and Ghoshal (1998) define social capital as *"the sum of actual and potential resources embedded within, available through, and derived from the network of relationships possessed by an individual or social unit"*. Social capital is associated with positive effects on knowledge sharing, cooperative behavior, team performance and success of IT projects (e.g., Borgatti and Foster 2003; George et al. 2014). Third-party developers, who interact with each other and organize themselves in platform-dedicated online communities, have the opportunity to build social capital. Clan control and social capital are both based on social relationships and therefore social capital may be a particularly pertinent concept to investigate means to facilitate the exercise of clan control (Kirsch et al. 2010). Indeed, a clan can be defined as a group with strong social capital (Chua et al. 2012). While previous studies have analyzed social capital as an antecedent of clan control, their focus was predominantly on corporate projects and downstream performance effects were neglected (Chua et al. 2012; Kirsch et al. 2010). Our study thus attempts to contribute to control and social capital literature by examining the facilitating role of social capital in shaping clan control in a more open and dynamic platform context and by investigating the resulting effects of clan control on crucial developer outcomes.

Nahapiet and Ghoshal (1998) divide social capital into three dimensions, which are the structural, the cognitive and the relational dimension of social capital. We conceptualize social capital in our study as a high-order representation of commonly applied sub-constructs of each dimension. The structural dimension of social capital is associated with the connections or social links between individuals (i.e., the quantity of relations). They serve as channels to exchange information (Tsai and Ghoshal 1998) and represent the potential resources of an individual or a group (Nahapiet and Ghoshal 1998). Despite the pure existence and number of social ties, Granovetter (1973) describes tie strength to reflect the intensity and frequency of social interactions through social links. Social interaction in social networks, such as software platform communities, occurs through posting, reading and responding to messages and information shared on the platform, which creates a social link between these individuals or the community as a collective actor (Wasko and Farja 2005). Third-party developers generally interact with other developers on the platform. Developers on a software platform are likely to establish strong structural social capital by frequently spending time on the platform and in its community regarding their development projects. They read and respond in developer forums, chats, wikis and blogs while developing their apps and they participate in platform activities like chats, conferences and meetings.

The cognitive dimension of social capital represents a common understanding and social identification among individuals which is necessary to engage in any kind of meaningful knowledge exchange (Nahapiet and Ghoshal 1998). We conceptualize cognitive social capital with the sub-constructs shared language and shared vision, which are critical in providing a shared understanding (Chiu et al. 2006; Nahapiet and Ghoshal 1998). Shared language can be defined as the extent to which group members are able to communicate with other members via shared symbol (Hutchins and Hazlehurst 1995). Regarding online communities, a shared language is especially important, given that interactions in an online context rely heavily on written language (Haythornthwaite 2007; Tsai and Ghoshal 1998). A shared vision comprises collective goals and common interests of group members which raises the probability of individuals to share information with each other (Tsai and Ghoshal 1998). Third-party developers on software platforms who use common terms or jargons regarding app development (e.g., programming languages, frameworks and development procedures) and use similar patterns of communication in discussion forums can therefore be considered to have strong cognitive social capital. Moreover, developing and adopting a shared vision and similar ambitions (e.g., on how development should be conducted or design and security standards) strengthens a mutual understanding and brings developers closer together.

The relational dimension of social capital refers to the personal relationships between individuals that have developed over time and therefore reflects the quality of social relations in a group (Nahapiet and Ghoshal 1998). With a strong relational social capital, individuals see themselves as an essential part of a collective (Nahapiet and Ghoshal 1998). We conceptualize relational social capital with the constructs trust, commitment and reciprocity, in line with previous research (Adler and Kwon 2002; Wasko and Farja 2005). Trust can be defined as the willingness of one party to be vulnerable to the actions of another party (Mayer et al. 1995) and describes an individual's belief in the integrity, benevolence and competence of the other party (McKnight et al. 2002). Trust is associated with creating and maintaining a relationship, given that trust leads to a higher willingness to engage in cooperative actions (Nahapiet and Ghoshal 1998; Wasko and Farja 2005). Commitment can be defined as a duty or obligation to engage in future actions (Colemann 1990). When individuals feel a strong sense of commitment, not only to other individuals but also to a collective, it is more likely that they feel obligated and contribute to the group themselves (Wasko and Farja 2005). Reciprocity refers to actions that depend on rewarding reactions from others (Blau 1964). Individuals in a group expect that after they have done something for the group, someone will do something for them in return. They feel a moral obligation to give something back to the group (Putnam 1993). Third-party developers who believe in the trustworthiness of other developers, who feel a sense of commitment and loyalty to a platform's community and who support each other are likely to develop relational capital on the platform. Platform developers with a strong relational social capital therefore may help other developers with their development problems, are more willing to ask for support and will be more open to share information on specific development tasks.

5.3 Research Model and Hypotheses

In this section, we develop our research model. We propose that building developers' social capital on software platform will facilitate the exercise of clan control and that clan control, in turn, enhances developers' performance and app success. We first develop hypotheses linked to the relationship between social capital and clan control (H1a, H1b, H1c), followed by the effects of clan control on app developers' project performance (H2a, H2b) and app success (H3a, H3b). Our research model is shown in Figure 5-1.

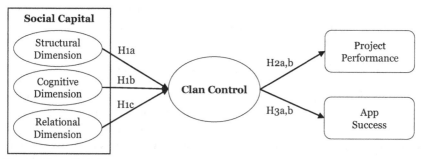

Figure 5-1: Research Model

5.3.1 Social Capital as Facilitator of Clan Control

Structural social capital in a collective provides access to information and resources through social interaction ties (Tsai and Ghoshal 1998) which are essential for collective collaborations (Burt 1992). Frequent interaction and communication with group members and regular participation in the group activities build such social interaction ties (Wasko and Farja 2005). In order to successfully promulgate and spread shared norms, values and common goals, social interactions between group members are indispensable. Ouchi (1979) noted that the dissemination of information is an important prerequisite for clan control and Turner and Makhija (2006) stated that frequent interactions and communication are required for the formation of clan control. A clear, frequent and wide-reaching communication is important for developing shared norms, values and common goals as well as a cooperative behavior (Stewart and Gosain 2006). Individuals with a high structural social capital are more likely to contribute information, share knowledge and utilize provided material of group members (De Dreu and West 2001; Robert et al. 2008). Individuals with more social ties than others and who are more centrally embedded are more likely to understand and adopt norms and expectations of a group (Rogers and Kincaid 1981). Structural social capital also enables group members to encourage others to behave according to shared norms and values and inspire others with common visions and goals (Kirsch et al. 2010).

Applied to the software platform setting, developers are more likely to spread, receive and adopt information on the platform when they have access to the platform, to the platform's community and to individual developers. This in turn is likely to build shared norms, values and common goals through frequent interactions and participation on the platform. Conversely, developers who refuse to interact with others and ignore platform-related activities are likely to build up less structural social capital. Thus, developers are unlikely to receive, understand and adopt the platform's norms, values and common goals. As such, the structural position of developers on a software platform should influence the likelihood of recognizing and understanding the norms, values and common goals of a platform and its community, which in turn supports the exercise of clan control. Taken together, these arguments suggest that:

Hypothesis 1a: Structural social capital facilitates the exercise of clan control.

Cognitive social capital refers to the common understanding and social identification among group members (Nahapiet and Ghoshal 1998). A shared language and shared visions enable individuals to engage in meaningful communication in a group and allow them to interpret and understand shared information and knowledge in a similar way as others (Wasko and Farja 2005). Clan control is characterized by promulgating, developing and spreading shared norms, values and common goals among group members (Kirsch 1997). In order to successfully exercise clan control, individuals ought to recognize and understand shared norms, values and common goals in similar ways. A shared language helps individuals to gain access to information and to evaluate the meaning and benefits of such information in a similar way, including social and work-related values, norms and common goals (Nahapiet and Ghoshal 1998). Individuals who are able to recognize and comprehend shared understandings are more likely to encourage other group members to adopt similar norms, values, goals and behaviors and contribute to building a clan (Kirsch et al. 2010). Shared visions, like common interests and collective goals, bring group members closer together and help them to see the meaning of sharing information (Cohen and Prusak 2001). Group members are more likely to understand and adopt collective understandings of norms, values and common goals, leading to common behaviors and outcomes, if they already share similar interests and beliefs (Chiu et al. 2006).

Taken to the platform context, third-party developers who share a common language (e.g., terms and jargons regarding app development on a specific platform) are more likely to recognize and understand shared values, norms and common goals on a platform. Additionally, developers who already share common interests and beliefs as a shared vision are more likely to adapt, share and encourage other developers to behave in accordance to new norms, values and common goals. This may include developing high-quality apps or offering a wide variety of free apps. Contrariwise, developers who do not fully understand shared information and discussions in the community and who have conflicting ambitions are unlikely to recognize, understand and spread shared norms, values and goals. Thus, they may hinder the implementation of clan control. Regarding these arguments, we believe that cognitive social capital supports the formation of clan control and the building of a clan on a platform. Hence, we hypothesize:

Hypothesis 1b: Cognitive social capital facilitates the exercise of clan control.

Relational social capital refers to the quality of a personal relationships between individuals in a collective (Nahapiet and Ghoshal 1998) that strongly facilitates and motivates cooperative actions and participation in a group (Colemann 1990). Strong relationships are driven by trusting beliefs, commitment and a norm of reciprocity of individuals in a collective (Wasko and Farja 2005). Ouchi (1979) argues that relationships among team members are a social prerequisite of clan control. With a strong relational social capital, individuals see themselves as an essential part of the group and feel a strong connection which commonly facilitates collaborative actions, knowledge sharing and more regular interactions (Nahapiet and Ghoshal 1998). Trust enables individuals to be more open to exchange information (Adler and Kwon 2002). According to Kirsch et al. (2010), individuals are more likely to attempt to influence others and individuals are more likely to react to such attempts with mutual trust and obligations in a collective. Correspondingly, an individual who is trusted and acts in mutuality is more likely to obtain information from other individuals in a collective (Tsai and Ghoshal 1998). Commitment to a group is important in order to develop and sustain agreed upon behaviors which reflects shared norms, values and common goals. Thus, individuals are not only committed to the group but also develop commitment to the group's norms, values and goals (Wasko and Farja 2005). Hence, social and work-related behaviors are more likely to be adjusted to shared norms, values and common goals of the group when individuals have a strong relational social capital.

In a software platform context, developers who feel a great deal of commitment to a platform community, who believe in the trustworthiness of other developers and who behave mutually are more likely to attempt to understand and spread the platform's norms, values and common goals. They as well are more likely to encourage others to behave in consistency with these shared beliefs. On the contrary, developers who are not trusted and do not trust others, who are not committed to the platform and do not help others on a platform are unlikely to receive, develop and adopt shared norms, values and common goals of the platform. Taken together, we believe that relational social capital facilitates the formation of clan control and the building of a clan on a platform. Hence we suggest that:

Hypothesis 1c: Relational social capital facilitates the exercise of clan control.

5.3.2 Performance Outcomes of Clan Control

Two critical outcome criteria on software platforms are third-party developers' project performance and the resulting success of their apps in the platform marketplace. These criteria not only contribute to the overall health of a software platform ecosystem (Hartigh et al. 2006), but also reflect app users' and developers' satisfaction towards a platform. We conceptualize developers' project performance adopted from information systems development literature with two constructs (Patnayakuni et al. 2007): While process performance denotes whether development projects typically finish within budget and schedule, output performance refers to the reliability of developed apps and user satisfaction with offered apps. Second, we conceptualize app success on platforms in two ways: First, as app quality, which is reflected in the average app rating of the app portfolio of developers (qualitative success) and second, as app adoption, mirrored in the average number of installations of developers' apps (quantitative success).

Clan control is exercised by promulgating shared values, norms and beliefs and by reducing different views across individuals, either by the controller or by individuals of the clan (Choudhury and Sabherwal 2003; Kirsch 1997; Rowe and Wright 1997). Clan control is realized when members of a clan have internalized the controller's goals and strategies through shared norms and values and therefore behave consistent with the controller's expectations. Moreover, clan control has reached its purpose when clan members embrace these shared values, adopt similar problem-solving approaches and commit to common goals (Ouchi 1979). Therefore, to the extent that platform owners emphasize and spread norms, values and goals that are beneficial for the platform (e.g., app development or maintenance techniques that attract customers), developers who have inherited these values and goals are not only more likely to achieve higher process and output performance, but also to produce higher-quality apps that are higher rated and downloaded more often.

Further, members of a clan openly discuss issues and questions and freely share information and knowledge, which results in collaboration and mutual learning (Gopal and Gosain 2010). In a collaborative collective, individuals are more likely to ask for help and are more open to share their expertise and knowledge (Nahapiet and Ghoshal 1998). If developers follow common goals, they are more likely to share best practices and problem solutions regarding app development in order to achieve a common goal. When communication and knowledge sharing in a clan is improved, actions will most likely result in less errors and reworks (Keil et al. 2013). Best-practice solutions may also concern work-related values and norms regarding coding and design standards, testing processes and framework usage. Developers who are part of a clan are therefore able to benefit from the competence and expertise of other developers, which is likely to enhance their process performance through fewer mistakes and less rework, which in turn may also improve the quality of their apps. Taken together, these arguments suggest that:

Hypothesis 2a: The exercise of clan control is positively related to developers' process performance.

Hypothesis 2b: The exercise of clan control is positively related to developers' output performance.

Hypothesis 3a: The exercise of clan control is positively related to app quality.

Hypothesis 3b: The exercise of clan control is positively related to app adoption.

5.4 Research Methodology

5.4.1 Data Collection and Sample Description

To test our hypotheses, we developed and conducted an online survey with developers of Google's Android platform. The Android platform was introduced for mobile app development by Google Inc. in 2008 and is a typical two-sided software platform which incorporates an operating system, middleware and applications. The platform is mostly free and aims at a wide range of different devices. A Software Development Kit as a programming interface enables third-party developers to develop apps for Android devices and to publish them via the Google Play Store, the Amazon App-Shop or even without an app store (Bergvall-Kåreborn and Howcroft 2011). By Q4/2014, the Google Play Store offered 1.43 million apps from nearly 400,000 developers and the Amazon App-Shop over 293,000 apps from nearly 50,000 developers. Android holds a market share of 76.6% and had 60% more app downloads in Q4/2014 compared to Apple apps (AppFigures 2015; IDC 2015). We thus believe that Android developers serve as a suitable representative for the mobile app market and for collecting data in our study.

Consistent with previous surveys of app developers (Benlian et al. 2015), we ran a self-developed web-crawler which randomly collected contact data from Android's app developers and data from their offered apps on the Google Play Store. A link to the online questionnaire was sent via mail to about 10,000 developers. The survey invitation and the start page of the survey included the purpose of the research study and ensured confidentiality and anonymity. Recipients were further asked to forward the questionnaire to their lead developer who may serve as a key informant (Kumar et al. 1993). Participants could win a tablet, an e-book reader or amazon gift-cards as a reward. 723 developers started our survey, resulting in a common response rate in such settings of 7.23%. After dropping cases with incomplete data and missing values, we removed additional 13 cases because of (1) a too short completion time and (2) because we could not assuredly match survey cases with the crawled app data from the Play Store. This resulted in a total of $N=218$ valid cases. Nonresponse bias was assessed by verifying that early and late respondents did not significantly differ (Armstrong and Overton 1977). The sample was compared based on its descriptives and responses to the study's main constructs. T-tests between the means of the early and late respondents did not reveal any significant differences ($p > 0.05$), indicating that nonresponse bias is unlikely to have a major role in our study.

App developers in our study were mainly self-employed with an own app development studio (42.3%) or hobbyist and private app developers (34.5%). Most developers have more than 7 years of experience in general software development (57.7%) and between 1 and 5 years of experience particular in app development (77.7%). Participants in our sample have developed 10.04 apps on average for the Android system and 6.51 apps for other platforms, while 52.3% have developed for Android only. The average size of the app portfolio was 6.95, i.e. the number of apps offered by the same developer or development studio in the Google Play Store. Descriptive statistics are shown in Table 5-1.

Table 5-1: Sample Descriptives (N = 218)

Experience in softw. development	Experience in app development	Current employment regarding app development	Average developed apps for...
< 1 year 6.8%	< 1 year 9.5%	Employed (company) 19.1%	... Android 10.04
1–3 years 16.4%	1–3 years 45.9%	Independent/freelancer 4.1%	... Apple 3.57
3-5 years 10.5%	3-5 years 31.8%	Hobbyist or private 34.5%	... Windows Phone 1.47
5-7 years 8.6%	5-7 years 9.5%	Self-employed 42.3%	... Blackberry 1.47
> 7 years 57.7%	> 7 years 3.2%		Total Average 16.55

5.4.2 Measurement Variables and Model

Prior to this research, we conducted interviews with 8 developers of the Android platform and the online gaming platform Steam, who are responsible for lead development. We interviewed them about how they work for the platform, how they interact with other developers, how they perceive their relation to fellow developers and the platform owner, and how they perceive different regulations from the platform owner. We also analyzed general policies and the terms and conditions published by platform owners from a control theory lens, including the different forms of control. Based on these results, survey items were adapted to the study's platform context based on established measures from existing scales in literature. Refined items were again evaluated in a survey pre-test phase to ensure the items were interpreted unambiguously and had high content and face validity. All latent constructs in the survey instrument were measured reflectively. In line with previous studies (Karahanna and Preston 2013), we modelled our social capital dimension as formative second-order hierarchical latent variables that combine the reflective constructs from prior studies as sub-constructs (first-order constructs) under the general concept of their respective social capital dimension (second-order constructs). With this modelling approach, we were able to better represent the level of abstraction of the social capital concept along with a more theoretical parsimony and reduction of model complexity (Becker et al. 2012).

We measured structural social capital with the social interaction ties construct based on three items of Hsiao and Chiou (2012). Even though we measured structural social capital with only one construct, we modeled a second-order construct for model consistency reasons.

Table 5-2: Construct Measures

Construct	Items
Social Interaction (Hsiao and Chiou 2012)	I frequently interact with other developers of the Android platform (e.g., forums, chats, blogs).
	I regularly participate in developer activities of the Android platform (e.g., live chats, online/offline meetings, conferences)
	I frequently read and inform myself on the Android platform (e.g., guidelines, tools, newsletters).
Shared Language (Chiu et al. 2006)	Developers of the Android community use common terms or jargons.
	Developers of the Android community use understandable communication pattern during discussions.
	Developers of the Android community use understandable narrative forms to post messages or articles.
Shared Vision (Tsai and Ghoshal 1998)	I share the same ambitions and visions with other developers of the Android platform.
	I am enthusiastic about pursuing the collective goals and mission of the Android platform.
Trust (Hsiao and Chiou 2012)	I feel that developers on the Android platform are trustworthy.
	I think that developers on this platform behave in a consistent manner.
	I think that developers on this platform will not take advantage of others even when the opportunity arises.
Commitment (Wasko and Farja 2005)	I would feel a loss if the Android platform and its community was no longer available.
	I really care about the fate of the Android platform and its community.
	I feel a great deal of loyalty to the Android platform and its community.
Reciprocity (Wasko and Farja 2005)	I believe that developers of the Android platform would help me if I need help.
	I know that other developers of the Android community will help me, so it's only fair to help other developers.
Clan Control (Kirsch et al. 2002)	* I attempt to be a regular member of the platform community.
	I attempt to understand the platform's goals, values and norms.
	I place a significant weight on understanding the platform's goals, values and norms.
	I actively participate in developer forums, channels or conferences to understand the platform's goals, values and norms.
Process Performance (Patnayakuni et al. 2007)	Our (or my) app development projects finish within budget.
	Our app development projects finish in schedule.
	Users are satisfied with the lead time of our app delivery.
Output Performance (Patnayakuni et al. 2007)	Users are satisfied with our developed apps.
	Apps that have been developed by us have a high reliability.
	Users are satisfied with the overall quality of our developed apps.

Note: All items were measured using a 7-point Likert scale, anchored at (1) = strongly disagree and (7) = strongly agree.
* Dropped due to low factor loading (<0.6)

For cognitive social capital, we included two first-order constructs, namely shared language based on three items of Chiu et al. (2006) and shared vision based on two items of Tsai and Ghoshal (1998). For relational social capital we included three first-order constructs which are trust, commitment and reciprocity. We based the trust construct on three items of Hsiao and Chiou (2012) who measured perceived trust in a virtual community. Commitment was based on three items of Wasko and Farja (2005) in order to capture commitment to the platform and its community. We measured reciprocity with two items based on Wasko and Farja (2005) to capture if developers in the community would help each other. As mentioned before, clan control has been differently conceptualized and operationalized in IS research (Chua et al. 2012; Kirsch et al. 2010). We adapted the measurement of clan control based on individual's perception of the exercise of clan control (Kirsch et al. 2002) with four items. The items analyze if developers attempt and put effort into becoming a part of the platform's community (i.e., the clan) by attempting to understand and placing a significant weight on understanding the platform's goals, norms and values as well as their participation in the clan and attempt to become a regular member (Kirsch et al. 2002). Process performance and output performance where both based on information systems development performance measures of Patnayakuni et al. (2007) with three items for each construct. App success was measured with objective data collected with our crawler software. App quality was measured with the average rating of a developer's app portfolio, while app adoption was captured with the average number of app downloads. In order to account for alternative explanations, control variables were included in the measurement. These are developers' years of experience in app development and the developers' app portfolio size in Google Play Store. The study's main constructs and measures are reported in Table 5-2.

5.5 Data Analysis and Results

In order to test our hypotheses, we used structural equation model (SEM) with partial least squares (PLS). PLS allows for testing the measurement model (i.e., the psychometric properties of the measurement scales) and the estimation of the structural model (i.e., the strength and direction of the relationship between the variables) simultaneously (Chin 1998). PLS has an added advantage over covariance-based methods (e.g., LISREL) in that it (1) maximizes the explained variance of endogenous variables in the structural model, which enables to understand the amount of variance explained in the constructs and (2) PLS does not make distributional assumptions for the data (Chin 1998). We used the software SmartPLS 2.0.M3 (Ringle et al. 2005). For robust PLS calculation, a minimum sample size of ten times the maximum number of any paths in the model is suggested (Hair et al. 2012), which our data exceeded with N=218. For assessing the significance levels of the paths, we used a bootstrapping procedure with no sign changes and 1,000 resamples following recommendations by Hair et al. (2012). For modelling the hierarchical structural model, we used the repeated indicator approach mode B with formative measures for the second-order dimensions, following guidelines by Becker et al. (2012). With a two-step approach, we first assessed our measurement model and then analyzed our research hypotheses.

5.5.1 Measurement Model Assessment

For measurement model assessment, we examined all latent reflective constructs regarding content validity, convergent validity and discriminant validity. Content validity was established by performing a qualitative pre-test to check for ambiguities, which resulted in some minor wording changes. We evaluated convergent validity with three criteria of Fornell and Larcker (1981): Factor loadings must load significantly and exceed the threshold value of .70; composite reliabilities should exceed .80; average variance extracted (AVE) must be above .50 (i.e., above the variance due to measurement error). All item loadings were significant (p < .001) and exceeded the recommended threshold value (See Table 5-3). All constructs' composite reliabilities exceeded .814 and all values for AVEs were above .595. Therefore, all study constructs fulfill the norms for convergent validity.

Table 5-3: Reliability, validity, and distribution statistics of latent variable scores

		Mean	Standard Deviation	Loading Range	Composite Reliability	Average Variance Extracted
1	Social Interaction	3.64	1.30	0.723 - 0.841	0.814	0.595
2	Shared Language	4.99	1.14	0.777 - 0.902	0.890	0.730
3	Shared Vision	4.34	1.53	0.916 - 0.923	0.916	0.845
4	Trust	4.52	1.12	0.769 - 0.901	0.878	0.706
5	Commitment	5.18	1.58	0.851 - 0.935	0.922	0.798
6	Reciprocity	5.33	1.28	0.920 - 0.920	0.917	0.847
7	Clan Control	5.17	1.31	0.851 - 0.912	0.918	0.790
8	Process Performance	5.17	1.14	0.801 - 0.863	0.865	0.682
9	Output Performance	5.64	0.98	0.874 - 0.914	0.925	0.804
10	App Quality	4.00	0.78	Single-item		
11	App Adaption	87,766	376,127	Single-item		

Regarding discriminant validity, AVE's square root should exceed the shared variance between a construct and all other constructs of the model (Fornell and Larcker 1981). As the factor correlation matrix in Table 5-4 indicates, all inter-correlations between the latent variables are lower than the square root of the AVE (shown in bolded cells). Therefore, the study constructs represent theoretically and empirically distinguishable concepts. Additionally, the Harman's single-factor test was performed to test for common method bias (Podsakoff et al. 2003). The results showed that a single factor could not account for the majority of the variance among the model variables and therefore did not result in any serious threats for our constructs. The first factor explained 22.48% of the variance and is thus significantly below the critical threshold value of 50%. For the second-order formative constructs, we assessed the weights and their statistical significance of the first-order constructs in forming their latent variables, as suggested by (Becker et al. 2012). However, there are no recommended threshold values for indicator weights for formative constructs (Chin 1998). Regarding the indicator associated with structural social capital, social interaction had a positive significant weight ($\beta = .99$, $p < .001$). For cognitive social capital, shared vision had a positive significant weight ($\beta = .88$, $p < .001$), while shared language was significant at the 10% level ($\beta = .20$, $p < .10$). For relational social capital, commitment and reciprocity had significant weights of ($\beta = .69$, $p < .001$) and ($\beta = .41$, $p < .05$) respectively, while the weights of trust were not significant on the relational dimension ($\beta = .12$, $p > .10$).

Table 5-4: Square root of AVE (bolded cells) and correlations of latent variable scores

		1	2	3	4	5	6	7	8	9	10	11
1	Social Interaction	**0.77**										
2	Shared Language	0.31	**0.85**									
3	Shared Vision	0.42	0.49	**0.92**								
4	Trust	0.27	0.32	0.34	**0.84**							
5	Commitment	0.31	0.33	0.49	0.49	**0.89**						
6	Reciprocity	0.42	0.46	0.48	0.40	0.36	**0.92**					
7	Clan Control	0.47	0.31	0.48	0.27	0.39	0.31	**0.89**				
8	Process Performance	0.17	0.32	0.29	0.27	0.20	0.16	0.33	**0.83**			
9	Output Performance	0.27	0.3	0.24	0.19	0.25	0.24	0.32	0.48	**0.90**		
10	App Quality	0.14	0.01	0.10	0.06	0.07	0.02	0.19	0.09	0.13	-	
11	App Adaption	0.12	0.04	-0.01	0.05	0.01	0.05	0.04	0.03	0.05	0.04	-

5.5.2 Hypotheses Testing

The structural model successfully explained a considerable proportion of variance in clan control ($R^2 = .34$) and smaller portions of variance in process performance ($R^2 = .11$), output performance ($R^2 = .10$) and app quality ($R^2 = .04$). Regarding path coefficients, there was a positive and significant effect of structural social capital on clan control ($\beta = .28$; $p < .001$), of cognitive social capital on clan control ($\beta = .26$; $p < .001$) and of relational social capital on clan control ($\beta = .18$; $p < .05$). Consequently, we found support for our hypotheses H1a, H1b and H1c.

Regarding the effects of clan control on project performance and app success, we found a positive and significant effect of clan control on process performance ($\beta = .33$; $p < .001$), of clan control on output performance ($\beta = .32$; $p < .001$) and on app quality ($\beta = .19$; $p < .01$). However, there was no significant effect of clan control on app adoption ($\beta = .04$; $p > .10$). Therefore we found support for hypothesis H2a, H2b and H3a, while H3b had to be rejected. Results of the model are shown in Figure 5-2.

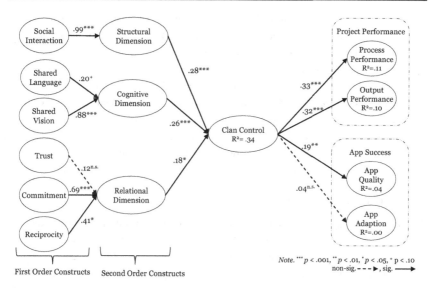

Figure 5-2: Results of Research Model

We also analyzed a full model including our control variables in order to control for alternative explanations. Still, our main results remained robust. Developers' experience in app development did not significantly influence clan control, process performance, app quality or app adoption (all p > .10). However, developers' experience had a positive significant effect on output performance (β = .22; p < .01). The effect of app portfolio size was non-significant on clan control, output performance, app quality and app adaption (all p > .10). Nonetheless, it had a positive significant effect on process performance (β = .16; p < .05). The explained variance in process performance and output performance increased slightly due to the effect of the control variables to (R^2 = .14), and (R^2 = .15) respectively.

5.5.3 Post-Hoc Analysis

In addition to our main analysis, we ran a post-host analysis to better understand the direct effects of social capital on our dependent variables and the mediating effect of clan control, following recommendations by Preacher and Hayes (2008). In the first step, we included the paths from each social capital dimension to each dependent variable, while removing the paths from clan control. We found positive significant effects from the structural dimension on output performance (β = .14; p < .05) and on app quality (β = .13; p < .05). Also, we found significant positive effects from the cognitive dimension on process performance (β = .29; p < .001) and on output performance (β = .18; p < .01). All other paths were non-significant (all p > .05). In the second step, we re-included clan control into our model in order to analyze its mediating effects. The effects from each social capital dimension on clan control remained significant. Regarding clan control, the effects on process performance and app quality remained significant, the effect on outcome performance marginal significant (p < .10) and on app adaption not significant. The effects from the structural dimension on output performance and on app quality as well as from the cognitive dimension on output performance became non-significant (all p > .05). Therefore, clan control fully mediated the effects on these dependent variables. Furthermore, the effect from the cognitive dimension of social capital on process performance decreased but remained significant (β = .23; p < .01), which implies a partial mediation.

5.6 Discussion and Conclusion

The aim of this study was to investigate whether clan control on software platforms can be facilitated with social capital in order to enhance the performance and success probability of third-party developers. Although software platforms are characterized by a highly dynamic and unstructured environment with a myriad of developers and numerous development projects, which makes it difficult to exercise tight control on every development project compared to traditional software development contexts, little is known about how especially clan control may be facilitated. Moreover, knowledge about how clan control affects developers' performance outcomes is limited. We examined whether social capital (i.e., structural, cognitive and relational social capital) positively affects clan control in a mobile app platform context and how clan control eventually translates into crucial performance outcomes. Three key findings can be derived from the results of our study.

First, we could demonstrate that social capital indeed positively facilitates the exercise of clan control. All three dimensions of structural, cognitive and relational social capital had a positive and significant effect on clan control. If developers have a strong social capital, it is more likely to successfully implement clan control on a software platform. A strong social capital may be manifested due to having frequent interactions with other developers, share a common language and a common vision (e.g., regarding development procedures, programming languages and development purposes), and being committed and behave mutually in the ecosystem with its community. Conversely, developers with a weak social capital are less likely to understand and develop shared norms, values and common behaviors on a platform and therefore will be less probable to be brought onto a common path and join a platform's clan.

Second, we could show that exercising clan control has a positive and significant effect on project performance as well as on the user ratings of their apps on the platform store. To the extent that third-party developers place a significant weight on understanding the platform's goals, values and norms, and actively keep track of changes (e.g., via developer forums, online communities and conferences), developers are more likely to incorporate the platform's common behaviors into their development and programming endeavors. This may result in higher project performance and app quality. Contrary to our hypothesis, our study results could not show an effect of clan control on app adoption in terms of the number of installations.

Third, some interesting insights can be derived from our post-hoc mediation analysis. All significant effects of the social capital dimensions on our dependent variables were fully or partially mediated by clan control. As such, the full potential and power of social capital can be leveraged and passed through to developers' performance outcomes only by implementing and exercising clan control on the platform. This again demonstrates the critical role of clan control as a governance mechanism on software platforms, given that the underlying effect of social capital on project performance outcomes can be explained with the exercise of clan control.

However, the explained variances of the endogenous variables in our structural model are rather small, revealing a tension between our theoretical development and the study's results. As an explanation, the model has only single paths to each endogenous variable and other factors we did not account for may have overridden effects of clan control. In order to get a deeper understanding of clan control on software platforms, and to maximize the model's explanatory power, future studies are advised to analyze if the rather low explained variance of our result model is also prevalent in other contexts. Future studies could also include additional constructs that may lead to higher performance outcomes.

Alongside to our key findings, other results are worthy to be further discussed. In previous studies on social capital, trust has been seen as an important sub-construct for relational social capital to enable knowledge sharing and a cooperative behavior among a collective (e.g., Nahapiet and Ghoshal 1998; Wasko and Farja 2005). However, trust in our study does not appear to have any influence on exercising clan control on a software platform. From a theoretical perspective, given that trust can lead to a commitment (Chua et al. 2012) and given the strong correlation between our trust and commitment construct (0.49), trust may be overridden by commitment. From a practical perspective, another explanation may be that developers in a community of a software platform, who usually have a high level of autonomy, do not put much thought into trusting each other, and that commitment to the platform and helping each other is more important for a relationship between developers. Further studies may have a deeper look into the trusting beliefs of third-party developers and their commitment to a platform in order to shed light on the relationships between developers and the developer community. In a similar way, shared language was only significant on a 10% level and therefore seems to play only a minor role in explaining cognitive social capital, which also calls for further research. Moreover, our study revealed that relational social capital had a weaker effect on clan control compared to the cognitive and structural dimension. Therefore, some social capital dimensions may be more important than others in facilitating the exercise of clan control on software platforms, which also offers further research opportunities.

5.6.1 Theoretical and Practical Implications

The findings of our study provide numerous implications for theory and practice. From a theoretical standpoint, our study offers a deeper understanding on how the exercise of clan control on a software platform may be facilitated and strengthened. Our study demonstrates that all three dimensions of social capital are positively related to the exercise of clan control and therefore building social capital serves as an important predictor of clan control in a software platform context. While our findings could verify previous findings on social capital and clan control (Chua et al. 2012; Kirsch et al. 2010), our study could further demonstrates that these positive effects of social capital on clan control are carried over to enhance developers' performance outcomes and that even in—if not especially in—decentralized and complex multi-project software development contexts, such as a software platform, social capital plays a central role in facilitating clan control.

We are therefore contributing to the body of knowledge about the potential of social capital and its power to explain social and organizational phenomenon in a yet underexplored platform context (Borgatti and Foster 2003; Nahapiet and Ghoshal 1998). Further, our study contributes to control theory (Kirsch 1997; Ouchi 1979) by investigating and demonstrating how the exercise of clan control may be facilitated and how clan control enhances crucial developers' outcomes in the light of the previously mentioned research gaps. Even more, our study could show that clan control can serve as a mediator, transmitting the positive effects of social capital to developers' performance and app quality, which, to the best of our knowledge, has not yet been investigated in IS research. This is even more important, given the hitherto underexplored effects of informal control modes in general and on software platforms in particular. We are therefore responding to research calls to analyze how dynamic and fast-growing platform ecosystems may be governed (Tiwana et al. 2013; Wareham et al. 2014). We are doing so by demonstrating how clan control, as an integral part of platform governance, operates on software platforms, could be strengthened by building developers' social capital and how clan control ultimately influences developers' behaviors and outcomes.

Our results also have interesting implications for platform owners and third-party developers. First, our study suggests that platform owners should increasingly focus on exercising clan control in order to positively influence developers' behaviors and outcomes on a platform while maintaining the platform's integrity. Clan control may be exercised by promulgating shared norms, values and common goals which are beneficial for the platform and by serving as an example for desired social and work-related behaviors. Platform owners could, for example, selectively participate in the developer community and promulgate goals, beliefs and market strategies of the platform through regular newsletters, developer publications and conferences. Common goals and beliefs may for example relate to the innovativeness of a platform, expected app designs and quality levels, openness and freedom of the platform, or characteristics of the targeted customer base. Second, our study findings underscore the need of building social capital to facilitate the exercise of clan control and ultimately to enhance developers' outcomes. Platform owners therefore are advised to support developers in building their social capital in the developer community by providing a platform ecosystem which simplifies communication and collaboration between developers. Developer forums, chats and conferences as well as solution-oriented wikis and blogs may help developers to interact with each other and to build social relations with individuals of the developer community. Third, app developers who aim at developing successful apps for a platform are advised to understand the platform's norms, values and common goals and to incorporate these into their development efforts. Closely following and inheriting shared values and common behaviors on a platform might not only help developers to become part of a platform clan that provides support, but also lead to better project performance and higher app quality.

5.6.2 Limitations and Future Work

While our study provides important contributions to both research and practice, we acknowledge several limitations that have to be considered when interpreting our results and implications. First, we focused our study on Android developers and our survey was mostly completed by self-employed or hobbyist developers. Therefore, results of our study may not be representative for other platforms, like the Apple App Store or Facebook's App Center, or for employed app developers. Future studies may examine a broader view of different software platforms with a larger mix of professional and hobbyist app developers and also compare effects across various platforms. Second, given the numerous studies on social capital and various ways of its conceptualization, we could only focus on key constructs for each dimension. While our constructs are well supported by literature, other constructs of social capital may be analyzed in future studies. Additionally, the three social capital dimensions are commonly seen as being dependent on each other (Colemann 1990; Granovetter 1973). However, for the sake of parsimony, we did not include these relations in our model, which offers potential for further research. Third, there are different research streams on clan control (Chua et al. 2012) and there is not yet an established and agreed upon measurement for clan control (Kirsch et al. 2010). While we believe that our measurement captured the exercise of clan control appropriately for our research purpose, other measurements may be applied and developed in future studies in order to better understand how clan control operates on software platforms. In this respect, complementary qualitative research (e.g., based on the grounded theory approach) would be a fertile avenue for future research to explore social capital instantiations more deeply in the app development context (e.g., Mahnke et al. 2015). Fourth, measures of process and outcome performance were adopted from a study with system development managers and may be biased in a single person developer context. We therefore recommend a cross validation with other measures in future studies. Fifth, we are aware that the structural model in our study explained only a low amount of variance in our depended variables. While the study focus was to analyze the effects of clan control, many other factors influence development performance and app success. Future studies are advised to take additional factors into account and analyze the structural model in other contexts. This may be developers' motivation, satisfaction, knowledge and competence, company size of the development studio, the popularity of app genres, marketing and pricing strategies for published apps, as well as other market forces on software platforms. Also, a fruitful avenue for future research may be studying the effects of social capital on portfolios of formal and informal control modes, given that typically a variety of controls are simultaneously exercised. Finally, our research model may be further expanded by including other variables that may be influenced by clan control and developers' social capital, like developers' attitudes and intentions, their creativity and innovativeness or the platform's overall stability and growth.

5.6.3 Conclusion

Given the myriad of third-party developers on software-based platforms and their numerous development projects, the question arises of how platform providers may successfully influence and steer these development projects and enhance platform performance and sustainability. Owing to the increasing importance of informal control modes in platform contexts, we analyzed how social capital facilitates the implementation and exercise of clan control and its resulting effects on crucial developer performance outcomes. By integrating social capital theory and control literature, results of our study suggest that all three dimensions of social capital (i.e., structural, cognitive and relational social capital) positively affects the implementation of clan control, which, based on our study, ultimately leads to higher development performance and app success on the platform. We believe that examining informal control modes in relation with social aspects of the developer community in platform settings is a rich avenue for further research. We hope that this study could provide new ideas and future directions on how IS research on platform governance and control could be further advanced.

Chapter 6: Thesis Conclusion

6.1 Summary of Key Findings

This thesis was motivated by the growing importance of software platforms for the software industry, arising novel governance challenges for platform providers and our limited understanding in IS research regarding control modes on software platforms. The purpose of this thesis was to understand how and why different control modes on software platforms affect third-party developers and how the exercise of promising control modes may be facilitated. In this regard, three studies were conducted, published across four scientific articles, which investigated control modes on software platforms with different foci and methodological approaches. These studies provided several findings, theoretical insights and contributions. The key findings of each article are briefly summarized in the following.

The **first article** (chapter 2) focused on identifying and categorizing existing control mechanisms on mobile software platforms in order to achieve a basic understanding of which control mechanisms are actually exercised on software platforms. We found that Apple and Google have increasingly employed informal control modes in their platform ecosystems. This finding encouraged us to further focus on the effects of particular informal control modes. We also reported first results of our experimental lab study for a practitioner audience, in which we found that self-control, compared to formal control, could lead to higher app quality and higher intention to stay on such software platforms.

In the **second article** (chapter 3), the full laboratory experiment is reported, in which we simulated a software platform development context wherein participants were exposed to different control modes. The study findings provided evidence for the superior effects of self-control compared to formal control modes in strengthening developers' app quality and platform stickiness. Developers who can freely choose and regulate their development procedures and outcomes are more likely to produce higher quality outcomes and are more willing to stay in such contexts. Further, the study revealed that developers' perceived autonomy provides a central explanatory mechanism for why self-control has stronger and more positive effects compared to formal control. Developers' higher autonomy under self-control is translated into enhanced developer outcomes and behaviors and therefore mediated the effects of self-control. Finally, the study results could not demonstrate differential effects of formal and self-control on developers' work efforts. However, a higher perception of autonomy influenced developers' efforts, which in turn positively affected their app quality.

The study in the **third article** (chapter 4) was conducted to analyze the downstream effects of informal control modes in an actual mobile software platform setting with a particular focus on the mediating role of third-party developers' intrinsic motivation. The study results revealed that both informal control modes (i.e., self- and clan control) have a positive influence on developers' intrinsic motivation. This implied that developers who perceive their decisions and activities more originated by themselves and who regularly interact and share common norms, values and goals with a platform and its community are more likely to have a higher intrinsic motivation to develop apps for the platform. In addition, the study showed that clan control is more conducive in shaping developers' intrinsic motivation compared to self-control. Second, we found support that intrinsic motivation significantly enhances developers' efforts, quality of their apps in the platform store as well as their intention to stay on the platform. Third and most important, the study demonstrated that intrinsic motivation partially and fully mediates the effects of self- and clan control on developers' effort and intention to stay on the platform. Developers' intrinsic motivation thus served as an important explanatory argument for why these positive effects of self- and clan control occur on software platforms.

The purpose of the **last article** (chapter 5) was to investigate whether clan control may be facilitated with third-party developers' social capital in order to enhance their performance outcomes on the platform. The study findings showed that each dimension of social capital significantly and positively affects the exercise of clan control on software platforms. In particular, it is more likely to successfully implement clan control if third-party developers have strong social capital with the platform's community. Social capital is in turn manifested by having frequent interactions with other developers, sharing a common language and vision regarding app development, and by behaving mutually and committed to the platform and its community. Further, successfully exercised clan control positively influenced third-party developers' project performance and quality of their apps. Therefore, if third-party developers place a significant weight on understanding the platform's goals, values and norms, and attempt to be a regular member of the platform community, they are more likely to incorporate the platform's common behaviors into their development and programming activities, which in turn may ultimately lead to better outcomes. Moreover, clan control fully or at least partially mediated the effects of the social capital dimensions on these endogenous variables, which provided again support for the importance of clan control in such settings.

6.2 Theoretical Contributions

This thesis was guided by three principal research questions, concerning how control modes affect third-party developers' crucial development outcomes and behaviors, how these effects may be explained and how promising control modes may be facilitated. Overall, the thesis' studies were able to provide a deeper understanding on how control modes operate on software platforms and how they affect third-party developers in such dynamic contexts. Following next, the main contributions are discussed regarding the thesis' research questions.

Referring to research question *RQ1*, concerning how control modes affect third-party developers' outcomes and behaviors, each study was able to contribute meaningful insights. In the first study, we could show that self-control compared to formal control is more conducive in influencing third-party developers' intention to stay on a platform, their app quality and their perceived autonomy. In the second study, we could provide evidence that self-control and clan control positively affect developers' intrinsic motivation as well as their development effort and intention to stay on the platform. Therefore, we were also able to reproduce previous findings from the laboratory experiment in a field study with higher external and ecological validity. Additionally, the study findings demonstrate that clan control is more conducive in influencing developers' intrinsic motivation and their development effort. Finally, the last study revealed that clan control is able to enhance third-party developers' project performance and app quality in the platform's market store, thus again providing evidence for the positive effects of informal control on software platforms.

Regarding *RQ2*, questioning why specific control effects occur on software platforms, study 1 and 2 were able to provide meaningful results. First, we could show that third-party developers' perceived autonomy serves as a mediator carrying the positive effects of self-control, compared to formal control, over to developers' app quality and intention to stay. Second, study 2 reveals that developers' intrinsic motivation is able to explain why self-control and clan control positively affect developers' project performance and intention to stay on the platform. Thus, we could show that developers' perceived autonomy and intrinsic motivation, which are constructs of self-determination theory, could provide explanations for why particularly informal control modes positively function on software platforms.

Finally regarding *RQ3*, the last study demonstrates how the exercise of clan control, a control mode that was previously considered to be important and promising for software platforms, could be facilitated. It is third-party developers' social capital that could serve as a predictor and facilitator for successfully exercising clan control on software platforms.

Overall, these findings highlight the importance of informal control modes on software platforms regarding their positive effects on crucial third-party developers' outcomes and behaviors. The thesis not only reveals how informal control modes affect third-party developers, but also why these effects occur (i.e., because of developers' perceived autonomy and intrinsic motivation) and how especially clan control can be facilitated based on developers' social capital. The thesis therefore answers to several research calls on analyzing and explaining how control modes operate in dynamic and complex multi it-project software platform settings (Ghazawneh and Henfridsson 2013; Tilson et al. 2012; Tiwana et al. 2013; Wareham et al. 2014). While control theory is reasonably advanced in organizational and project-related contexts with a strong focus on the nature, antecedents and choice of control modes, our knowledge regarding the governance of software platforms ecosystems is rather scarce (Tiwana et al. 2013). By studying effects of previously neglected informal control modes in a yet underexplored context, the thesis' findings therefore significantly contribute to control theory (Kirsch 1997; Ouchi 1979) and platform governance literature (Tiwana et al. 2010; Tiwana et al. 2013). Moreover, Maruping et al. (2009) called for research concerning contingencies under which self-control could lead to positive outcomes for project quality, for which this thesis was able to provide some insights regarding software platform contexts. The thesis further contributes to motivation and self-determination literature (Deci and Ryan 2002; Locke and Latham 2004), by providing insights on how developers' perceived autonomy and intrinsic motivation could mediate and explain the effects of informal control modes in software platform settings. Given that social capital could facilitate the exercise of clan control, the thesis also contributes to the body of knowledge regarding the potential of social capital (Borgatti and Foster 2003; Nahapiet and Ghoshal 1998). Finally, the results further emphasize that high performance outcomes and beneficial behaviors are possible even without traditional tight formal control and therefore also contributes to an ongoing discussion about "more control is better" (Tiwana et al. 2010).

6.3   Practical Contributions

Besides the theoretical contributions, the thesis findings also provide interesting recommendations and guidelines for software platform providers and third-party developers. Platform providers may use the studies' results to understand how and why control modes on software platforms affect third-party developers' project performances, app quality and intentions to stay on a platform. This could enable platform owners to carefully decide on exercising different control modes based on the platform's goals and objectives. Regarding the thesis' results, platform providers are advised to increasingly exercise informal control modes and find areas where such forms of control are applicable on their platform. The thesis could show that even without exercising conventional tight formal control, high performance outcomes and positive developer behaviors for the platform ecosystem are conceivable. Platform owners should therefore exercise more soft-power instruments, i.e. self- and clan control, instead of traditional hard-power instruments such as financial incentives or sanctions (Yoffie and Kwak 2006). For self-control, platform owners may encourage and support third-party developers in exercising self-control on their work processes and outcomes by structuring the platform environment appropriately and by providing open access to crucial development and market statistics which are necessary for making strategic decisions. Platform providers may also provide IT tools, documentations and trainings as well as examples for best-practice behaviors which could help developers in making decisions. In order to exercise clan control, platform providers may focus on bringing third-party developers onto a common path and encourage them to consider shared norms, values and common goals which are beneficial for the platform, including a compelling platform vision. They are advised to promulgate such shared norms, values and common goals by participating in developer communities and spread desired platform goals, beliefs and market strategies with newsletters, publications for developers or dedicated developer conferences. In addition, in order to shape a strong platform community or clan, platform owners are advised to support developers in building their social capital by providing developer forums, chats and conferences as well as solution-oriented wikis and blogs, which may help developers to interact with each other and to build social relations with individuals of the developer community.

Third-party developers who are eager to maximize their autonomy and intrinsic motivation are advised to choose software platforms in which predominately informal control modes are exercised. Such more open and self-regulating governance structures may enhance their outcome quality and performance as well as their willingness to stay on the platform, which in turn decreases possible switching costs. Additionally, app developers who aim at developing successful apps for a platform are advised to understand the platform's norms, values and common goals and to incorporate these into their development efforts. Closely following and inheriting a platform's shared values and common behaviors might not only help developers to become part of a platform clan, but also lead to better performance outcomes.

6.4 Limitations and Future Research

Despite the thesis' contributions to research and practice, some limitations have to be considered when interpreting the findings and implications. First, the studies were conducted in the context of mobile software platforms with Android app developers in the survey studies. Thus, generalizability may be limited to such contexts. Future studies may analyze control modes across different mobile platforms, such as the ecosystems around Apple's App Store or Microsoft's Windows Phone Store, and also across non-mobile software platforms, like the Facebook App Center. A comparison regarding the perceptions and effects of different control modes across various software platforms including a broad mix of professional and private developers offers fruitful and promising research avenues. Second, we analyzed control modes merely as dichotomous, mutually exclusive governance strategies at a single point in time without considering dependencies and interaction effects of control modes in typical control portfolios. Future studies may investigate the complementary or substitutive effects of combined control modes and additionally include changes in governance characteristics over time into a longitudinal study. Third, while we considered various important alternative explanations across the thesis' studies, there are factors we did not account for. Similarly, some rather small explained variances in the structural models may be due to other factors overriding the effects of control modes. Future studies may extend the thesis' research models by including additional factors in order to gain a deeper understanding of interactive effects and to maximize the models' explanatory power. These may be third-party developers' extrinsic motivation, trust in the platform vendor, their overall attitude and satisfaction towards and with the platform as well as their creativity and innovativeness in developing apps. Furthermore, third-party developers' marketing and pricing strategies, software platforms' financial attractiveness and competitive intensity as well as its overall stability and growth may further shed light on crucial outcomes and behaviors of third-party developers. These future research opportunities may further contribute to our understanding regarding the effects of control modes in software platform contexts and may therefore advance IS control research and platform governance literature beyond the current body of knowledge.

References

Adler, P.S., and Kwon, S.-W. 2002. "Social Capital: Prospects for a New Concept," *Academic Management Review* (27:1), pp. 17-40.

Agarwal, R., and Karahanna, E. 2000. "Time Flies When You're Having Fun: Cognitive Absorption and Beliefs About Information Technology Usage," *Management Information Systems Quarterly* (24:4), pp. 665-694.

Amabile, T.M. 1998. "How to Kill Creativity," *Harvard business review* (76:5), pp. 76-87.

Amabile, T.M., Goldfarb, P., and Brackfleld, S.C. 1990. "Social Influences on Creativity: Evaluation, Coaction, and Surveillance," *Creativity Research Journal* (3), pp. 6-21.

Amabile, T.M., Hill, K.G., Hennessey, B.A., and Tight, E.M. 1994. "The Work Preference Inventory: Assessing Intrinsic and Extrinsic Motivational Orientations," *Journal of Personality and Social Psychology* (66:5), pp. 950-967.

AppFigures. 2015. "App Stores Growth Accelerates in 2014." Retrieved March 31, 2015, from http://blog.appfigures.com/app-stores-growth-accelerates-in-2014/

Apple. 2014. "App Store Sales Top $10 Billion in 2013. Record-Breaking December with over $1 Billion in Sales." Retrieved July 21, 2014, from http://www.apple.com/pr/library/2014/01/07App-Store-Sales-Top-10-Billion-in-2013.html

Apple. 2015. "App Store Rings in 2015 with New Records." Retrieved February 2, 2015, from http://www.apple.com/pr/library/2015/01/08App-Store-Rings-in-2015-with-New-Records.html

Armstrong, J.S., and Overton, T.S. 1977. "Estimating Nonresponse Bias in Mail Surveys," *Journal of Marketing Research* (14), pp. 396-402.

Bandura, A. 1997. *Self-Efficacy: The Exercise of Control*. New York: Macmillan.

Basole, R.C., and Karla, J. 2011. "On the Evolution of Mobile Plattform Ecosystems Structure and Strategy," *Business & Information Systems Engineering* (3:5), pp. 313-322.

Becker, J.-M., Klein, K., and Martin, W. 2012. "Hierarchical Latent Variable Models in Pls-Sem: Guidlines for Using Reflective-Formative Type Models," *Long Range Planning* (45:5-6), pp. 359-394.

Benlian, A., and Hess, T. 2007. "A Contingency Model for the Allocation of Media Content in Publishing Companies," *Information & Management* (44:5), pp. 492-502.

Benlian, A., Hilkert, D., and Hess, T. 2015. "How Open Is This Platform? The Meaning and Measurement of Platform Openness from the Complementors' Perspective," *Journal of Information Technology* (30:3), pp. 209-228.

Bergvall-Kåreborn, B., and Howcroft, D. 2011. "Mobile Applications Development on Apple and Google Platforms," *Communications of the Association for Information Systems* (29).

Bergvall-Kåreborn, B., Howcroft, D., and Chincholle, D. 2010. "Outsourcing Creative Work: A Study of Mobile Application Development," *International Conference on Information Systems (ICIS) 2010*, St. Louis, Missouri, USA.

Blau, P.M. 1964. *Exchange and Power in Social Life*. New York: John Wiley and Sons.

Borgatti, S.P., and Foster, P. 2003. "The Network Paradigm in Organizational Research: A Review and Typology," *Journal of Management* (29:6), pp. 991-1013.

Boudreau, K.J. 2012. "Let a Thousand Flowers Bloom? An Early Look at Large Numbers of Software App Developers and Patterns of Innovation," *Organization Science* (23:5), pp. 1409-1427.

Boudreau, K.J., and Lakhani, K.R. 2009. "How to Manage Outside Innovation," *MIT Sloan Management Review* (50:4), pp. 69-76.

Burkhard, C., Widjaja, T., and Buxmann, P. 2012. "Software Ecosystems," *Business & Information Systems Engineering* (4:1), pp. 41-44.

Burt, R.S. 1992. *Structural Holes*. Cambridge, MA: Harvard University Press.

Campbell, J.P., and Pritchard, R.D. 1976. "Motivation Theory in Industrial and Organizational Psychology," in *Handbook of Industrial and Organizational Psychology*, M.D. Dunnette (ed.). Chicago, IL: Rand McNally, pp. 63–130.

Cardinal, L.B. 2001. "Technological Innovation in the Pharmaceutical Industry: The Use of Organizational Control in Managing Research and Development," *Organization Science* (12:1), pp. 19-36.

Carton, J.S. 1996. "The Differential Effects of Tangible Rewards and Praise on Intrinsic Motivation: A Comparison of Cognitive Evaluation Theory and Operat Theory," *The Behavior Analyst* (19:2), pp. 237-255.

Ceccagnoli, M., Forman, C., Huang, P., and Wu, D.J. 2012. "Cocreation of Value in a Platform Ecosystem: The Case of Enterprise Software," *Management Information Systems Quarterly* (36:1), pp. 263-290.

Chin, W.W. 1998. *The Partial Least Squares Approach for Structural Equation Modelling*. Hillsdale, NJ: Lawrence Erlbaum Associates.

Chin, W.W., and Todd, P.A. 1995. "On the Use, Usefulness, and Ease of Use of Structural Equation Modeling in Mis Research: A Note of Caution," *Management Information Systems Quarterly* (19), pp. 237-237.

Chiu, C.-M., Hsu, M.-H., and Wang, E.T.G. 2006. "Understanding Knowledge Sharing in Virtual Communities: An Integration of Social Capital and Social Cognitive Theories," *Decision Support Systems* (42:3), pp. 1872-1888.

Choudhury, V., and Sabherwal, R. 2003. "Portfolios of Control in Outsourced Software Development Projects," *Information Systems Research* (14:3), pp. 291-314.

Christen, M., Iyer, G., and Soberman, D. 2006. "Job Satisfaction, Job Performance, and Effort: A Reexamination Using Agency Theory," *Journal of Marketing* (70:1), pp. 137-150.

Chua, C.E.H., Lim, W.K., Soh, C., and Sia, S.K. 2012. "Enacting Clan Control in Complex It Projects: A Social Capital Perspective," *Management Information Systems Quarterly* (36:2), pp. 577-600.

Churchill, G.A., Ford, N.M., Hartley, S.W., and Walker Jr, O.C. 1985. "The Determinants of Salesperson Performance: A Meta-Analysis," *Journal of Marketing Research* (22:2), pp. 103-118.

Claussen, J., Kretschmer, T., and Mayrhofer, P. 2013. "The Effects of Rewarding User Engagement: The Case of Facebook Apps," *Information Systems Research* (24:1), pp. 186-200.

Cohen, D., and Prusak, L. 2001. *In Good Company; How Social Capital Makes Organizations Work*. Bosten, MA: Harvard Business School Press.

Cohen, J. 1988. *Statistical Power Analysis for the Behavioral Sciences*. Hillsdale, New Jersey: Lawrence Erlbaum Associates Inc.

Colemann, J.S. 1990. *Foundations of Social Theory*. Cambridge, MA: Belknap Press.

Das, T.K., and Teng, B.-S. 2001. "Trust, Control, and Risk in Strategic Alliances: An Integrated Framework," *Organization Studies* (22:2), pp. 251-283.

Davis, F.D., Bagozzi, R.P., and Warshaw, P.R. 1992. "Extrinsic and Intrinsic Motivatoin to Use Computers in the Workplace," *Journal of Applied Psychology* (22:14), pp. 1111-1132.

De Dreu, C.K.W., and West, M.A. 2001. "Minority Dissent and Team Innovation; the Importance of Participation in Decision Making," *Journal of Applied Psychology* (86:6), pp. 1191-1201.

Deci, E.L., Eghrari, H., Patrick, B.D., and Leone, D.R. 1994. "Facilitating Internalization: The Self-Determinaton Theory Perspective," *Journal of Personality* (62), pp. 119-142.

Deci, E.L., and Ryan, R.M. 1985. *Intrinsic Motivation and Self-Determination in Human Behavior*. New York: Plenum Press.

Deci, E.L., and Ryan, R.M. 1987. "The Support of Autonomy and the Control of Behavior," *Journal of Personality and Social Psychology* (53:6), pp. 1024-1037.

Deci, E.L., and Ryan, R.M. 2000. "The "What" and "Why" of Goal Pursuits: Human Needs and the Self-Determination of Behavior," *Psychological Inquiry* (11:4), pp. 227-268.

Deci, E.L., and Ryan, R.M. 2002. *Handbook of Self-Determination Research*. Rochester, NY: University of Rochester Press.

Eisenhardt, K.M. 1985. "Control: Organizational and Economic Approaches," *Management Science* (31:2), pp. 134-149.

Eisenmann, T., Parker, G., and Van Alstyne, M. 2011. "Platform Envelopment," *Strategic Management Journal* (32:12), pp. 1270-1285.

Fernandez, S., and Moldogaziev, T. 2012. "Using Employee Empowerment to Encourage Innovative Behavior in the Public Sector," *Journal of Public Administration Research and Theory* (23:1), pp. 155-187.

Fornell, C., and Larcker, D.F. 1981. "Evaluating Structural Equation Models with Unobservable Variables and Measurement Error," *Journal of Marketing Research* (18:1), pp. 39-50.

Gagne, M., and Deci, E.L. 2005. "Self-Determination Theory and Work Motivation," *Journal of Organizational Behavior* (26:4), pp. 331-361.

Gefen, D., Karahanna, E., and Straub, D.W. 2003. "Trust and Tam in Online Shopping: An Integrated Model," *Management Information Systems Quarterly* (27:1), pp. 51-90.

Gefen, D., and Straub, D.W. 2005. "A Practical Guide to Factorial Validity Using Pls-Graph: Tutorial and Annotated Example," *Communications of the Association for Information Systems* (16:1), pp. 91-109.

George, B., Hierschheim, R., and von Stetten, A. 2014. "Through the Lens of Social Capital: A Research Agenda for Studying It Outsourcing," *Strategic Outsourcing: An International Journal* (7:2), pp. 107-134.

Ghazawneh, A., and Henfridsson, O. 2013. "Balancing Platform Control and External Contribution in Third-Party Development: The Boundary Resources Model," *Information Systems Journal* (23:2), pp. 173-192.

Ghose, A., Goldfarb, A., and Han, S.P. 2012. "How Is the Mobile Internet Different? Search Costs and Local Activities," *Information Systems Research* (24:3), pp. 613-631.

Goldbach, T., and Benlian, A. 2015a. "How Informal Control Modes Affect Developers' Trust in a Platform Vendor and Platform Stickiness," in: *Proceedings der 12. Internationalen Tagung Wirtschafsinformatik*. Osnabrück, Deutschland.

Goldbach, T., and Benlian, A. 2015b. "How Social Capital Facilitates Clan Control on Software Platforms to Enhance App-Developers' Performance and Success," in: *Thirty Sixth International Conference on Information Systems (ICIS)*. Fort Worth, USA.

Goldbach, T., and Benlian, A. 2015c. "Kontrollmechanismen Auf Software-Plattformen," *HMD - Praxis der Wirtschaftsinformatik* (52:3), pp. 347-357.

Goldbach, T., and Benlian, A. 2015d. "Understanding Informal Control Modes on Software Platforms – the Mediating Role of Third-Party Developers' Intrinsic Motivation," in: *Thirty Sixth International Conference on Information Systems (ICIS)*. Fort Worth, USA.

Goldbach, T., and Kemper, V. 2014. "Should I Stay or Should I Go? The Effects of Control Mechanisms on App Developers' Intention to Stick with a Platform," in: *Twenty Second European Conference on Information Systems*. Tel Aviv, Israel.

Goldbach, T., Kemper, V., and Benlian, A. 2014. "Mobile Application Quality and Platform Stickiness under Formal Vs. Self-Control — Evidence from an Experimental Study," in: *Thirty Fifth International Conference on Information Systems (ICIS)*. Auckland, New Zealand.

Gopal, A., and Gosain, S. 2010. "The Role of Organizational Controls and Boundary Spanning in Software Development Outsourcing," *Information Systems Research* (21:4), pp. 960-982.

Granovetter, M.S. 1973. "The Strength of Weak Ties," *American Journal of Sociology* (78:6), pp. 1360-1380.

Gregory, R.W., Beck, R., and Keil, M. 2013. "Control Balancing in Information Systems Development Offshoring Projects," *Management Information Systems Quarterly* (37:4), pp. 1211-1232.

Gulati, R., Puranam, P., and Tushman, M. 2012. "Meta-Organization Design: Rethinking Design in Interorganization and Community Contexts," *Strategic Management Journal* (33:6), pp. 571-586.

Hackman, J.R., and Oldham, G.R. 1976. "Motivation through the Design of Work: Test of a Theory," *Organizational Behavior & Human Performance* (16:2), pp. 250-279.

Hagiu, A., and Halaburda, H. 2010. *Responding to the Wii? Hbs Case No. 709-448.* Boston: Harvard Business School.

Hair, J., Sarstedt, M., Ringle, C., and Mena, J. 2012. "An Assessment of the Use of Partial Least Squares Structural Equation Modeling in Marketing Research," *Journal of the Academy of Marketing Science* (40:3), pp. 414-433.

Hartigh, E., Tol, M., and Visscher, W. 2006. "The Health Measurement of a Business Ecosystem," in: *European Chaos/Complexity in Organisations Network (ECCON) annual meeting 2006.* Bergen aan Zee, Netherlands.

Haythornthwaite, C. 2007. "Social Networks and Online Communities," in *The Oxford Handbook of Psychology,* A. Joinson, K. McKenna, T. Postmes and U.-D. Reips (eds.). New York: Oxford University Press, pp. 121-138.

Helson, H. 1964. *Adaptation-Level Theory: An Experimental and Systematic Approach to Behavior.* New York: Harper & Row.

Henderson, J.C., and Lee, S. 1992. "Managing I/S Design Teams: A Control Theories Perspective. (Information System)," *Management Science* (38:6), pp. 757-777.

Hilkert, D., Benlian, A., and Hess, T. 2010. "Motivational Drivers to Develop Apps for Social Software-Platforms: The Example of Facebook," *AMCIS 2010 Proceedings, Paper 86,* Lima, Peru.

Hsiao, C.-C., and Chiou, J.-S. 2012. "The Effect of Social Capital on Community Loyalty in a Virtual Community: Test of a Tripartite-Process Model," *Decision Support Systems* (54:1), pp. 750-757.

Hu, L., and Bentler, P.M. 1999. "Cutoff Criteria for Fit Indexes in Covariance Structure Analysis: Conventional Criteria Versus New Alternatives," *Structural Equation Modeling* (6:1), pp. 1-55.

Hutchins, K.-Y., and Hazlehurst, B. 1995. "How to Invent a Lexicon: The Development of Shared Symbols in Interaction," in *Artificial Societies, the Computer Simulation of Social Life,* N. Gilbert and R. Conte (eds.). London: UCL Press, pp. 132-159.

Iansiti, M., and Levien, R. 2004a. *The Keystone Advantage: What the New Dynamics of Business Ecosystems Mean for Strategy, Innovation, and Sustainability.* Boston, MA, USA: Harvard Business Press.

Iansiti, M., and Levien, R. 2004b. "Strategy as Ecology," *Harvard Business Review* (82:3), pp. 68-81.

IDC. 2015. "Smartphone Os Market Share, Q4 2014." Retrieved March 31, 2015, from http://www.idc.com/prodserv/smartphone-os-market-share.jsp

Janowicz, M., and Noorderhaven, N. 2006. "Levels of Inter-Organizational Trust: Conceptualization and Measurement," in *Handbook of Trust Research,* B. Reinhard and A. Zaheer (eds.). Cheltenham, UK: Edward Elgar Publishing, Inc.

Jansen, S., Brinkkemper, S., and Finkelstein, A. 2009. "Business Network Management as a Survival Strategy: A Tale of Two Software Ecosystems," *1st International Workshop on Software Ecosystems, CEUR-WS vol. 505,* Virginia, USA.

Jaworski, B.J. 1988. "Toward a Theory of Marketing Control: Environmental Context, Control Types, and Consequences," *The Journal of Marketing* (52:3), pp. 23-39.

Jensen, M.C., and Meckling, W.H. 1976. "Theory of the Firm: Managerial Behavior, Agency Costs and Ownership Structure," *Journal of Financial Economics* (3:4), pp. 305-360.

Johnson, E.J., Bellman, S., and Lohse, G.L. 2003. "Cognitive Lock-in and the Power Law of Practice," *Journal of Marketing* (67:2), pp. 62-75.

Kanfer, R. 1990. "Motivation Theory and Industrial and Organizational Psychology," in *Handbook of Industrial and Organizational Psychology*, M.D. Dunnette and L.M. Hough (eds.). Palo Alto: Consulting Psychologists Press, pp. 75-170.

Karahanna, E., and Preston, D.S. 2013. "The Effect of Social Capital of the Relationship between the Cio and Top Management Team on Firm Performance," *Journal of Management Information Systems* (30:1), pp. 15-55.

Katz, M.L., and Shapiro, C. 1985. "Network Externalities, Competition, and Compatibility," *The American Enonomic Review* (75:3), pp. 424-440.

Katz, M.L., and Shapiro, C. 1994. "Systems Competition and Network Effects," *Journal of Economic Perspectives* (1:6), pp. 93-115.

Ke, W.L., and Zhang, P. 2009. "Motivations in Open Source Software Communities: The Mediating Role of Effort Intensity and Goal Commitment," *International Journal of Electronic Commerce* (13:4), pp. 39-66.

Keil, M., Rai, A., and Liu, S. 2013. "How User Risk and Requirements Risk Moderate the Effects of Formal and Informal Control on the Process Performance of It Projects," *European Journal of Information Systems* (22:6), pp. 650-672.

Kirk, R.E. 2012. *Experimental Design: Procedures for the Behavioral Sciences*, (4th ed.). Los Angeles, USA: Sage Publications Ltd.

Kirsch, L.J. 1996. "The Management of Complex Tasks in Organizations: Controlling the Systems Development Process," *Organization Science* (7:1), pp. 1-21.

Kirsch, L.J. 1997. "Portfolios of Control Modes and Is Project Management," *Information Systems Research* (8:3), pp. 215-239.

Kirsch, L.J. 2004. "Deploying Common Systems Globally: The Dynamics of Control," *Information Systems Research* (15:4), pp. 374-395.

Kirsch, L.J., Ko, D.-G., and Haney, M.H. 2010. "Investigating the Antecedents of Team-Based Clan Control: Adding Social Capital as a Predictor," *Organization Science* (21:2), pp. 469-489.

Kirsch, L.J., Sambamurthy, V., Dong-Gil, K., and Purvis, R.L. 2002. "Controlling Information Systems Development Projects: The View from the Client," *Management Science* (48:4), pp. 484-498.

Klarner, P., Sarstedt, M., Hoeck, M., and Ringle, C.M. 2013. "Disentangling the Effects of Team Competences, Team Adaptability, and Client Communication on the Performance of Management Consulting Teams," *Long Range Planning* (46:3), pp. 28-286.

Kohli, R., and Kettinger, W.J. 2004. "Informating the Clan: Controlling Physicians' Costs and Outcomes," *Management Information Systems Quarterly* (28:3), pp. 363-394.

Krippendorff, K. 2004. *Content Analysis: An Introduction to Its Methodology*. Beverly Hills, CA: Sage Publications.

Kumar, N., Stern, L.W., and J.C., A. 1993. "Conducting Interorganizational Research Using Key Informations," *The Academy of Management Journal* (36:6), pp. 1633-1651.

Li, D., Browne, G., and Wetherbe, J. 2006. "Why Do Internet Users Stick with a Specific Web Site? A Relationship Perspective," *International Journal of Electronic Commerce* (10:4), pp. 105-141.

Locke, E.A., and Latham, G.P. 2004. "What Should We Do About Motivation Theory? Six Recommendations for the Twenty-First Century," *Academic Management Review* (29:3), pp. 288-403.

Loiacono, E.T., Watson, R.T., and Goodhue, D.L. 2007. "Webqual: An Instrument for Consumer Evaluation of Web Sites," *International Journal of Electronic Commerce* (11:3), pp. 51-87.

Macstories. 2013. "The Numbers from Apple's Wwdc 2013 Keynote." Retrieved July 21, 2014, from http://www.macstories.net/news/the-numbers-from-apples-wwdc-2013-keynote/.

Mahnke, R., Benlian, A., and Hess, T. 2015. "A Grounded Theory of Online Shopping Flow," *International Journal of Electronic Commerce* (19:3), pp. 54-89.

Manikas, K., and Jansen, K.M. 2013. "Software Ecosystems - a Systematic Literature Review," *Journal of Systems and Software* (86:5), pp. 1294-1306.

Maruping, L.M., Venkatesh, V., and Agarwal, R. 2009. "A Control Theory Perspective on Agile Methodology Use and Changing User Requirements," *Information Systems Research* (20:3), pp. 377-399.

Mayer, R.C., David, J.H., and Schoorman, F.D. 1995. "An Integrative Model of Organizational Trust," *Academy of Management Journal* (20:3), pp. 709-734.

McKnight, D.H., Choudhury, V., and Kacmar, C. 2002. "Developing and Validating Trust Measures for E-Commerce: An Integrative Typology," *Information Systems Research* (13:3), pp. 334-359.

Muthén, L.K., and Muthén, B.O. 2010. *Mplus: Statistical Analysis with Latent Variables: User's Guide*. Muthén & Muthén.

Nahapiet, J., and Ghoshal, S. 1998. "Social Capital, Intellectual Capital, and the Organizational Advantage," *Academy of Management Review* (23:2), pp. 242-266.

Nidumolu, S.R., and Subramani, M.R. 2003. "The Matrix of Control: Combining Process and Structure Approaches to Managing Software Development," *Journal of Management Information Systems* (20:3), pp. 159-196.

Omodei, M.M., and Wearing, A.J. 1990. "Need Satisfaction and Involvement in Personal Projects: Toward an Integrative Model of Subjective Well-Being," *Journal of Personality and Social Psychology* (59:4), pp. 762-769.

Orlikowski, W.J. 1991. "Integrated Information Environment or Matrix of Control? The Contradictory Implications of Information Technology," *Accounting, Management and Information Technologies* (1:1), pp. 9-42.

Osterloh, M.B., and Frey, B. 2000. "Motivation, Knowledge Transfer, and Organizational Forms," *Organization Science* (11:5), pp. 538-550.

Ouchi, W.G. 1979. "A Conceptual Framework for the Design of Organizational Control Mechanisms," *Management Science* (25:9), pp. 833-848.

Ouchi, W.G. 1980. "Markets, Bureaucracies, and Clans," *Administrative Science Quarterly* (25:1), pp. 129-141.

Ouchi, W.G., and Price, R.L. 1978. "Hierarchies, Clans, and Theory Z: A New Perspective on Organization Development," *Organizational Dynamics* (7:2), pp. 24-44.

Patnayakuni, R., Rai, A., and Tiwana, A. 2007. "Systems Development Process Improvement: A Knowledge Integration Perspective," *IEEE TRANSACTIONS ON ENGINEERING MANAGEMENT* (54:2), pp. 286-300.

Pavlou, P.A., Liang, H., and Xue, Y. 2007. "Understanding and Mitigating Uncertainty in Online Exchange Relationshsips: A Principal-Agent Perspective," *Management Information Systems Quarterly* (31:1), pp. 105-136.

Pearce, C.L., Sims Jr, H.P., Cox, J.F., Ball, G., Schnell, E., Smith, K.A., and Trevino, L. 2003. "Transactors, Transformers and Beyond: A Multi-Method Development of a Theoretical Typology of Leadership," *Journal of Management Development* (22:4), pp. 273-307.

Podsakoff, P.M., MacKenzie, S.B., Lee, J.Y., and Podsakoff, N.P. 2003. "Common Method Biases in Behavioral Research: A Critical Review of the Literature and Recommended Remedies.," *Journal of Applied Psychology* (88:5), pp. 879-903.

Preacher, K.J., and Hayes, A.F. 2008. "Asymptotic and Resampling Strategies for Assessing and Comparing Indirect Effects in Multiple Mediator Models," *Behavior Research Methods* (40:3), pp. 879-891.

Putnam, R. 1993. "The Prosperous Community: Social Capital and Public Life," *The American Prospect* (13:4), pp. 35-42.

Reiter-Palmon, R., Mumford, M.D., and Threlfall, K.V. 1998. "Solving Everday Problems Creatively: The Role of Problem Construction and Personality Type," *Creativity Research Journal* (11:3), pp. 187-197.

Ringle, C.M., Wende, S., and Will, A. 2005. "Smartpls 2.0 (M3) Beta." Hamburg: SmartPLS. Retrieved from http://www.smartpls.com.

Robert, L.P., Dennis, A.R., and Ahuja, M.K. 2008. "Social Capital and Knowledge Integration in Digitally Enabled Teams," *Information Systems Research* (19:3), pp. 314-334.

Roberts, J.A., Hann, I.-H., and Slaughter, S.A. 2006. "Understanding the Motivations, Participation, and Performance of Open Source Software Developers: A Longitudinal Study of the Apache Projects," *Management Science* (52:7), pp. 984-999.

Rochet, J.-C., and Tirole, J. 2003. "Platform Competition in Two-Sided Markets," *Journal of the European Economic Association* (1:4), pp. 990-1029.

Rogers, E., and Kincaid, D. 1981. *Communication Networks: Towards a New Paradigm for Research.* New York: The Free Press.

Rowe, W.G., and Wright, P.M. 1997. "Related and Unrelated Diversification and Their Effect on Human Resource Management Controls," *Strategic Management Journal* (18:4), pp. 329-338.

Rustagi, S., King, W.R., and Kirsch, L.J. 2008. "Predictors of Formal Control Usage in It Outsourcing Partnerships," *Information Systems Research* (19:2), pp. 126-143.

Ryan, R.M. 1982. "Control and Information in the Intranpersonal Sphere: An Extension of Cognitive Evaluation Theory," *Journal of Personality and Social Psychology* (43), pp. 245-254.

Ryan, R.M., and Deci, E.L. 2000. "Intrinsic and Extrinsic Motivations: Classic Definitions and New Directions," *Contemporary Educational Psychology* (25:1), pp. 54-67.

Rysman, M. 2009. "The Economics of Two-Sided Markets," *Journal of Economic Perspectives* (23:3), pp. 125-143.

Sarstedt, M., and Wilczynski, P. 2009. "More for Less? A Comparison of Single-Item and Multi-Item Measures," *Die Betriebswirtschaft* (69:2), pp. 211-227.

Shah, S.K. 2006. "Motivation, Governance, and the Viability of Hybrid Forms in Open Source Software Development," *Management Science* (52:7), pp. 1000-1014.

Slocum, J.W., and Sims, H.P. 1980. "A Typology for Integrating Technology, Organization, and Job Design.," *Human Relations* (33:3), pp. 193-212.

Spreitzer, G.M. 1995. "Psychological Empowerment in the Workplace: Dimensions, Measurement, and Validation," *Academy of Management Journal* (38:5), pp. 1442-1465.

Srivastava, S., and Teo, T. 2012. "Contract Performance in Offshore Systems Development: Role of Control Mechanisms," *Journal of Management Information Systems* (29:1), pp. 115-158.

Stewart, K.J., and Gosain, S. 2006. "The Impact of Ideology on Effectiveness in Open Source Software Development Teams," *Management Information Systems Quarterly* (30:2), pp. 291-314.

Techcrunch. 2011. "Millions of People Became Facebook "Developers" Just for Timeline Access." Retrieved April 30, 2014, from http://techcrunch.com/2011/12/07/millions-of-people-became-facebook-developers-just-for-timeline-access/

Tilson, D., Lyytinen, K., and Sorensen, C. 2012. "Digital Infrastructures: The Missing Is Research Agenda," *Information Systems Research* (21:4), pp. 748-759.

Tiwana, A. 2010. "Systems Development Ambidexterity: Explaining the Complementary and Substitutive Roles of Formal and Informal Controls," *Journal of Management Information Systems* (27:2), pp. 87-126.

Tiwana, A. 2014. *Platform Ecosystems: Aligning Architecture, Governance, and Strategy.* Burlington, Massachusetts: Morgan Kaufmann.

Tiwana, A., and Keil, M. 2007. "Does Peripheral Knowledge Complement Control? An Empirical Test in Technology Outsourcing Alliances," *Strategic Management Journal* (28:6), pp. 623-634.

Tiwana, A., and Keil, M. 2009. "Control in Internal and Outsourced Software Projects," *Journal of Management Information Systems* (26:3), pp. 9-44.

Tiwana, A., Konsynski, B., and Bush, A.A. 2010. "Platform Evolution: Coevolution of Platform Architecture, Governance, and Environmental Dynamics (Research Commentary)," *Information Systems Research* (21:4), pp. 675-687.

Tiwana, A., Konsynski, B., and Venkatraman, N. 2013. "Special Issue: Information Technology and Organizational Governance: The It Governance Cube," *Journal of Management Information Systems* (30:3), pp. 7-12.

Tsai, W., and Ghoshal, S. 1998. "Social Capital and Value Creation: The Role of Intrafirm Networks," *The Academy of Management Journal* (41:4), pp. 464-476.

Turner, K.L., and Makhija, M.V. 2006. "The Role of Organizational Controls in Managing Knowledge," *Academic Management Review* (31:1), pp. 197-217.

Utman, C.H. 1997. "Performance Effects of Motivational State: A Meta-Analysis," *Personality and Social Psychology Review* (1), pp. 170-182.

Vallerand, R.J., and Bissonnette, R. 1992. "Intrinsic, Extrinsic, and Amotivational Styles as Predictors of Behavior: A Prospective Study," *Journal of Personality* (60:3), pp. 599-620.

Venkatesh, V., and Speier, C. 1999. "Computer Technology Training in the Work-Place: A Longitudinal Investigation of the Effect of Mood," *Organizational Behavior and Human Decision Processes* (79:1), pp. 1-28.

Wang, G., and Netemeyer, R.G. 2002. "The Effects of Job Autonomy, Customer Demandingness, and Trait Competitiveness on Salesperson Learning, Self-Efficacy, and Performance," *Journal of the Academy of Marketing Science* (30:3), pp. 217-228.

Wareham, J., Fox, P.B., and Cano Giner, J.L. 2014. "Technology Ecosystem Governance," *Organization Science* (25:4), pp. 1195 - 1215.

Wasko, M.M., and Farja, S. 2005. "Why Should I Share? Examining Social Capital and Knowledge Contribution in Electronic Networks of Practice," *Management Information Systems Quarterly* (29:1), pp. 35-57.

Weinberg, G. 1998. *The Psychology of Computer Programming. Silver Anniversary Edition.* New York: Van Nostrand Reinhold.

Wells, J.D., Valacich, J.S., and Hess, T.J. 2011. "What Signals Are You Sending? How Website Quality Influences Perceptions of Product Quality and Purchase Intentions," *Management Information Systems Quarterly* (35:2), pp. 373-396.

Wilde, M., Bätz, K., Kovaleva, A., and Urhahne, D. 2009. "Überprüfung Einer Kurzskala Intrinsischer Motivation (Kim)," *Zeitschrift für Didaktik der Naturwissenschaften* (15), pp. 31-45.

Yoffie, D.B., and Kwak, M. 2006. "With Friends Like These: The Art of Managing Complementors," *Harvard Business Review* (84:9), pp. 88-98.

Zott, C., Amit, R., and Donlevy, J. 2000. "Strategies for Value Creation in E-Commerce: Best Practice in Europe," *European Management Journal* (18:5), pp. 463-475.

Printed in the United States
By Bookmasters